What some have said about

A Biblical St:

The Christian faith is not something that we do on Sunday but its life and it's to be a continual growth. To accept Christ is to never stop wanting to be more like Christ in all we do. It's not just enough to say that we're on our way to heaven. People will say "I know the Lord and I'm on my way to heaven." That's not the issue now that you know Christ. The issue is "Are you becoming more like the one who's taking you to heaven? How many people are you taking to heaven with you? Are you growing spiritually? Are you becoming more like Christ? Are you building relationships? Are you making disciples? Those are the real issues.

My friend and brother in Christ, Darryl Allgood has done an excellent job in capturing this truth and sharing it in a personal and practical way through his journey as a Christian. I recommend that you read it and allow the Holy Spirit to speak to your heart and evaluate your relationship with Christ.

Daryel A. O'Barr
"Drawing The Net Ministries"
320 Santa Anita Ave
Woodstock, Ga. 30189
drawingthenet.org

*   *   *

As a Minister of Education, I am always looking for books to help new Christians to grow and walk in their faith. Darryl has done an excellent job of laying out a step by step plan for Christian growth. As you read through the chapters you will find the information to be helpful and encouraging. One of the most important parts of this book is to take the time at the end of the chapters as you reflect upon the chapter and what it means to you. Darryl Allgood has covered the basics of Christianity very well and it is up to us to apply these truths to our life. I hope that you enjoy this book as much as I did!

Mike Blount
Minister of Education
Faith Baptist Church
Monroe, Ga.

I have read this book multiple times and I am astounded at how much is packed in. This book provides a winning game plan and practical tools to all people on all spiritual levels. I have also read the "Rhymes For Times" section and they alone were a tremendous blessing. I highly recommend this book to read and give to others and you will be richly blessed.

Brian Widmer, Pastor, Christian Educator
Independent Missionary to the Youth of America

A Biblical Start to Solid Foundations is a clear and concise discipleship resource. It is a very useful tool to guide a new believer in the initial steps of his spiritual journey with Jesus Christ. I commend this book to all Christ followers seeking to fulfill our Lord's command to make disciples.

Pastor Jeff Box
Walker Baptist Church
Monroe, Georgia
Romans 1:16

A BIBLICAL START
—— TO ——
SOLID FOUNDATIONS

A Christian's Guide to Conquer, Overtake and Win the
Victories Through Struggles, Obstacles and Problems In
The Christian Life.

R. Darryl Allgood

WestBow
PRESS
A DIVISION OF THOMAS NELSON

WestBow Press books may be ordered through booksellers or by contacting:

WestBow Press
A Division of Thomas Nelson
1663 Liberty Drive
Bloomington, IN 47403
www.westbowpress.com
1-(866) 928-1240

Because of the dynamic nature of the Internet, any web addresses or links contained in this book may have changed since publication and may no longer be valid. The views expressed in this work are solely those of the author and do not necessarily reflect the views of the publisher, and the publisher hereby disclaims any responsibility for them.

Any people depicted in stock imagery provided by Thinkstock are models, and such images are being used for illustrative purposes only.

Certain stock imagery © Thinkstock.

ISBN: 978-1-4497-5606-2 (sc)
ISBN: 978-1-4497-5607-9 (hc)
ISBN: 978-1-4497-5605-5 (e)

Library of Congress Control Number: 2012910432

Scripture taken from the New King James Version. Copyright 1979, 1980, 1982 by Thomas Nelson, inc. Used by permission. All rights reserved.

Printed in the United States of America

WestBow Press rev. date: 06/26/2012

I consider it an honor to dedicate this book to my children in whom I love dearly and want no more than to see them seek God with their whole heart and life. I love each of you more today than ever before.

TABLE OF CONTENTS

INTRODUCTION

When we stop to think about the years that pass so quickly, we cannot help but count the people and families that have been affected by the simple fact they had no action plans or blueprints to follow. We have heard them ask "What do I do next?" or "What is the *New Life* as a Christian and child of God?", or "What do I do next or how do I handle this problem when it comes up in my life?" If you are like me, there have been many times you have asked or heard questions like this over and over, each time seeking answers from the scriptures to show and see what God has said and how He wants us to react when these events arise. After deep consideration and many hours, I felt compelled and led to sit down and put the scriptural plan and process on paper in this form. The Bible says in *Matthew 7:23-25, "Therefore whoever hears these sayings of Mine, and does them, I will liken him to a wise man who built his house on the rock: ²⁵ and the rain descended, the floods came, and the winds blew and beat on that house; and it did not fall, for it was founded on the rock."*

As I considered each chapter during the writing process, it seemed as though God was laying a foundation to have a structured building placed for eternity. That's exactly how we can see each chapter in this book; whether a New Christian, a Young Christian, or a long-time Christian that is going through valleys or dealing with issues that have weighted them down in bondage for years. All of us are human and; therefore, we will always find ourselves needing a solid foundation that will not be moved no matter what the problem or obstacle.

Changing your way of thinking after years of practice is difficult. Overcoming self-defeating behaviors is a struggle, and not easy to accomplish on our own. However, God has given us His Word and promise that it can be done in His strength. The only sure way to a Biblical and Solid Foundation is through Jesus Christ our Lord. *John 14:6, "Jesus said to him, "I am the way, the truth, and the life. No one comes to the Father except through me."* My prayer is that this book will enable, strengthen and enlighten your life as a Christian and child of God.

In the chapters to follow, each will end with a short summarizing time for you to reflect back on what you have read. This design is intended to reaffirm and help implement principles and truths that may be new to you. They will truly impact your life from today forward. You will reinforce them by writing them down and this activity will also assist in remembering the principles and truths as you go along. The foundation layer under construction now supports the additional layers that will come after and will build your fortress to stand without shaking. As you begin this journey of building in your life, stop and ask God to enable you to have a clear mind and to open it for fathomless opportunities for growth and wisdom. Ask the Holy Spirit to allow you understanding in better achieving these things in your own personal life. I promise that you will see and live a completely different life with God, such as you never thought possible.

CHAPTER 1

A NEW BIRTH

John 3:1-7

Chapter 1

THE NEW BIRTH

A man went to retrieve his paper one morning as his daily routine allowed, then went inside the house and sat with his coffee and began to read. Turning to the obituary section and scanning the names listed, his eyes doubled in size when he saw his own name listed with the others that had passed. He became outraged and immediately went to the phone and called the editor. As he began to describe his anger and how inexcusable this act was, he felt his blood pressure starting to rise. He exclaimed, "How could you do such a horrible thing?" The editor apologized deeply several times over but the man failed to accept his apology. The editor finally stated to the man, "This is what I am willing to do. Tomorrow, I will have your name placed in the New Birth section of the morning edition and you can have a brand new start". That is exactly what God does when He gives the spiritually dead life upon their asking Him to come into their hearts and lives; when they sincerely turn from the life of sin to the Savior. *Isaiah 1:18* says *"Come now and let us reason together, saith the Lord: though your sins be as scarlet, they shall be as white as snow".*

The New Birth we are referring to above is not that of a physical sense but of the spiritual one. In the passage of scripture above, Jesus told Nicodemus *"Verily, verily, I say unto thee, except a man is born again, he cannot see the kingdom of God."* Jesus goes on to tell Nicodemus that our physical bodies can only be born one time and that it is impossible to re-enter a mother's womb for a second birth. But we must be born again spiritually. The most important part of our life is making a decision on the destination of our spiritual soul. That is the part of us that is spiritually dead and, when we accept Christ, is reborn, making us a child of God. The choice of life is the quickening the Bible speaks of in *John 5:21. "For as the Father raises up the dead, and quickeneth them, even so the Son quickeneth whom he will."* Our life alone, as it stands, without God, is dead. He said, *"That which is born of flesh is flesh . . . ."* In other words, after so long, this flesh will get old and sickly and will eventually die away but that which is of the Spirit is spirit. It is the part of us we cannot see but feel deep inside of ourselves that makes us who we are.

You and I can look in the mirror and see ourselves as whom we were born to be. Have you looked across this land lately? You never see another you; even though there are millions and millions upon millions of people that are alive or that are deceased. God made you unique and your soul as well. When this body dies, and it will one day, where will the soul that was given to you by God go? In *Hebrews 9:27*, God said, *"And it is appointed unto men once to die, but after this the judgment . . ."* This is a warning to every person. *"But after this . . ."* is the clearest way to answer the question "What is next for you?" God is saying that, if you have the Holy Spirit, you have life in Him.

We are all familiar with the process that leads to a new birth. We see a man and a woman meet one another. They then fall deeply in love. After a time of dating and courtship, they get to know each other and finally decide to set a wedding date and get married. After they have been married for a time, the wife and husband find they are expecting their first child. As new parents, they are filled with joy and excitement beyond measure or description. How would you describe a new birth in your family? It is joy unspeakable at times and especially for the first time parent. As soon as the pregnancy is confirmed, you start to make preparations for the day this new life enters your home. It is a type of joyful work that will be rewarded in about nine months. The new birth in your family is one with distinct genes, hair color and looks. This is determined by the mother and father's unique composition. As the child starts to grow, we look to see if the traits are more from mom's side of the family or dad's. This, of course, is a normal and natural reaction. You may ask, "Why is this so important in a new Christian's life?" The answer to your question is that we have a physical heritage that goes all the way back to the day God created Adam and Eve. From that day all the way up until now, the human nature has followed each and every birth. Our spiritual heritage goes back to Adam and Eve as well. That is where you are right now. It brings us to the New Birth in Christ.

As a new Christian and as "A Child of God", you are truly as excited as the new parent is, but in a different sense. As the new parent is bragging about the child that has recently entered the family, you brag about your new life in Christ. You want the entire world to know about your Savior. You have just accepted Jesus Christ into your heart and you are a new Christian.

Many people feel that this new walk and what it entails will come naturally; but it does not. Remember back to a time where you were completely unlearned about a subject. There were the times of reading, studying and learning to be better informed or more aware of that specific subject. As a new Christian, it too will bring many times we must be enlightened about our daily living. Once a person has accepted Christ as their Savior, they are traveling on a new road on which they have never been before. They have begun a walk that will be brand new to them. It is the New Start that will transform every part of their being. This chapter will explain the new start of the Christian's life in several steps. As a person walks along the road of life, he or she will approach a point to where a decision must be made that is life or death. This person may choose to continue on the road one has traveled for many years simply because it is comfortable, even though it contains potholes, big rocks and a hunger that is never quenched. Or they may choose the new road with eternal life as the destination. If you are anything like me, you would love to have someone brief you on what's in store and help you to know how to handle life's upcoming curves and obstacles. In order for a New Start as a child of God, there are several things you must understand.

❖ *Who are the real sinners?*

The Bible tells us in *Psalms 51:5, "Behold, I was shaped in iniquity, and in sin did my mother conceive me."* In writing these inspired words, David said that we all were born in sin and there is something in every person that pulls them in the wrong ways. A child comes forth from the womb with a nature to "Get what I want." As parents, think back to when the baby was new and everyone wanted to hold him (or her). After a while, the baby enjoyed being held all the time and then, when you went to put him down, he let out this blood curdling cry. What happened can be agreed on by every parent in this world. The child made you think that something was wrong when, in reality; the child had been spoiled. Would you agree that the child has now learned how to lie to you? Well of course he has, because of the sinful nature we are all born with.

Now that we understand the nature we are born with, we can agree we are all sinners and cannot save ourselves. In *Romans 3:23*, the Bible said *"For all have sinned and come short of the Glory of God."* Also in *First John 1:9-10, "If we confess our sins, he is faithful and just to forgive us our sins and to cleanse us from all unrighteousness." If we say we have not sinned, we make him a liar and his word (the truth) is not in us."* We do not measure up and we come up short of perfection, which makes us sinners. It is like you and a few friends are trying out for a football team and the position they need to fill is quarterback. The coach has said, "You must throw the ball and hit a specific target." Everyone has now gripped the ball as best they can and given it their very best throw. You landed only one inch from the designated target and the others landed even closer to the target. Who wins the position? All of you were really close but no one hit the target dead center. The coach has made the decision and says, "That was a very good try and you all were really close but no one hit the mark, so no one qualifies for the team." If we give it our very best effort, we still come up short. That is because we all are human and we were born with that sinful nature. This is what separates us from God. When Adam and Eve first sinned, they broke the relationship that God intended to have between man and Himself. They passed on to every man, woman, boy and girl that same sinful nature. *Romans 5:12 "Wherefore, as by one man's sin entered into the world, and death by sin, and so death passed upon all men, for that all have sinned."* There was no death, no sickness, no pain or sin until the day when Adam and Eve disobeyed God. From that day forward, we have been infected with sin; it's in our blood. There is no way to get around it, above it or past it. It has created within us a hunger, not a physical hunger, but one of a spiritual nature that can only come through and from Jesus Christ, our Lord. Once the sin had been committed, it broke the direct line that God had intended to use to communicate and talk with us. We have been searching from that point on for the rekindling of that relationship. That is why Jesus had to come and die for you and for me; so that the relationship could be restored. Jesus said in *John 6:35, "I am the bread of life; He that cometh to me shall never hunger, and he that believeth on me shall never thirst."*

❖ *Who owes this penalty for Sin?*

We must also understand there is a penalty for sin, our sin. Sin has separated us from God and that is why there is an emptiness within us that can never be filled by things such as money, treasures, people or fame in this world—only by Him. The sin that now exists within our lives separates us from God and, unless the sin is removed, it is a huge barrier and will separate us from God for eternity. God said in *John 3:36, "He that believeth on the Son hath everlasting life; and he that believeth not the Son shall not see life, but the wrath of God abideth on him."* What does the Bible mean when it speaks of death? The Bible tells us there are two deaths we must endure. The first death is that of our physical body. The second death is the spiritual one, our soul. Our soul is what makes you and me who we are because of God's amazing ability to make each of us unique. The Bible speaks of our spiritual death as eternal separation from God. Let's reflect back onto the rich man and Lazarus in *Luke 16:19-31.* The rich man had everything he could physically desire before his physical death but, once his body had reached its physical end, his spiritual soul was carried into Hell because of his refusal of God's perfect plan. In Hell, the rich man lifted up his eyes and God allowed him to see Abraham far off. The rich man wanted Abraham to send Lazarus to him with just one drop of water to quench his tormenting thirst. Our bodies can only suffer like this if Hell is an actual place. The rich man's soul had physical sight and had to feel physical pain in order to have a physical thirst. The ultimate description of Hell is a physical one.

Some people may say, "I am not a sinner" or "I am not that bad of a person." At this point in my life, I have heard this statement many times in witnessing and soul-winning. However, we can only rely on what the Bible says in *1 John 1:8-9. "If we say we have no sin, we deceive ourselves and the truth is not in us."* You can disagree with people on many different subjects but, when it comes to God's word, the truth is the truth. We can look in *Romans 6:23* where it states *"For the wages of sin is death . . ."* A simple illustration of this would be that you have worked for the last two weeks at your job and it is now pay day. You will receive wages for what you are due or what is owed to you. That is the same explanation of this passage. Our sin has brought with it a debt and a pay day. There is no other way to explain it except to say that we are due a spiritual death like the rich man. Our debt of sin can only be paid by a substitution and that substitution was the Son of God. *John 3:16 "For God so loved the world that whosoever believeth in Him should not perish but have everlasting life."* The second part of that verse says *"BUT the gift of God is eternal life through Jesus Christ, our Lord."* The life-changing fact of this verse affirms that we have a free gift and that gift is eternal life through Jesus Christ, the son of God. This has changed everything. There is a free gift for you and for me but how do we actually receive this gift? When you have been presented a gift, no matter what it may be, you must first receive it. That is to say, you extend your hands, agree to receive the gift, and then you physically take it. You now have it in your possession, and it's yours. In order to receive the free gift of salvation, you must realize Jesus paid that debt of sin for you on the cross of Calvary. He was that perfect substitute for you and for me. To claim salvation for ourselves, we must simply accept this gift from Him.

❖ *The Acknowledgement of Sin:*

This now leaves us at the threshold of acknowledging and taking to heart several things. (1) Jesus died for your sin and mine. (2) God has raised Him from the dead on the third day and He ascended into heaven and He is seated on the right hand of God and (3) *I John 1:9, "If we confess our sins, He is faithful and just to forgive us our sins, and cleanse us from all our unrighteousness."* God's word then says, "Ye shall be saved." *Romans 10:9-13.* Our trust can only be in Jesus and in Him alone.

Let's say you have a brand new swing that has a look so breathtaking for its beauty just installed on your front porch. You look on with such awesomeness and just cannot believe its sight. Its design is for the sitting, swinging and supporting of you and me but you conclude it is too breathtaking to place yourself. Until you fully and completely place yourself in this swing, with all of its beauty and awesomeness, you have no trust in it at all therefore; you miss out on its purpose and design. Similarly, the debt of sin was carried by Jesus to Calvary and the burden of that sin debt is why He made that journey. Jesus agreed to relieve you and me of sins debt. Once you place complete trust in Christ as you do with the swing, Christ becomes your support and your anchor. He came to earth and went to Calvary and said, *"It's finished."* That means that nothing else can or must be done; our debt has been paid and we have been made righteous in God's sight through the Son of God. God's word tells us in *Romans 10:13, "For whosoever shall call upon the name of the Lord, shall be saved."* The word "shall" does not mean "maybe" or "possibly"; no, it is a 100%, "yes you are and yes I am". That is the icing on the cake. Once you have reached this point, there is nothing you can do but praise the Lord and thank Him for dying for you and me and creating a perfect way to heaven.

To summarize to this point: we are all sinners, sin has a debt and the debt was paid for by Jesus Christ. All we have to do is confess that sin and ask forgiveness and the Bible assures us we shall be forgiven and saved. Once you and I arrive at this point, where do we go from here?

❖ *Believe Jesus Alone Died For You And Me:*

God did not send His son for baptism, church membership or faithful church attendance but for the world. That is what the death, burial and resurrection of the son of God for all mankind is all about. That is what salvation truly means. You ask, *"How can I know that if I trust Jesus Christ as my Savior, I will go to Heaven?"* God does not and cannot lie. *Hebrews 6:18* and also *Titus 1:2* tells us it is impossible for God to lie. The worst sin a person ever commits is not trusting Jesus as their Savior. I agree with the man that said, *"God is too wise to be mistaken and too honest to deceive us."* In order to actually make your trust reality, you must confess with your heart and soul that you know Jesus died for you and that you want Him to remove sin from your heart and cleanse you from all unrighteousness. This is what is meant by asking Jesus to come into your heart and save you. Once you have done this, you are a child of God. That means that your name has been written in the Lamb's Book of Life. No matter where you go or what you may do, the blood of Jesus Christ has been applied to your heart and soul. That is the most important thing you could ever do, even if you have done nothing else. The Bible said in *Romans 10:11 "Whosoever believeth on Him shall not be ashamed."* Also *Acts 2:37-41, "Then they that gladly received his word were baptized: and the same day there were added unto them about three thousand souls."* This was the first Christian church and Peter told them to repent of their sin and be baptized. The most important thing to note is that baptism is not salvation! The act of being baptized is the outward sign of obedience to God's word. God teaches us to allow baptism to be our first step in obedience to him. It is an outward sign that we accept and profess what God has done for us. Following baptism, we start the growth process as a new child in Christ Jesus within the church.

This chapter is designed to confirm one's salvation and to show the only way to start a new life as a child of God. God's plan was and is perfect in all things. *Acts 4:12, "There is no other name given unto man whereby one must or can be saved."* If you have read this chapter and, for the very first time in your life, realized your need of the Savior then now, today, accept Christ as your one and only way to heaven. This simple prayer can be prayed right at this moment.

Dear Jesus;

I know that I am not perfect. I am a sinner and I cannot save myself. You are the only one who died for me and can wash my sins all away. I am asking you to forgive me and wash all my sins away. I want you to cleanse and make me whole and come into my heart to live. I trust you and you alone.

Thank you for saving me. I will be baptized as a sign that I do trust you as my God and Savior from now through eternity.

Once you have done this, your next step is to make a public profession declaring your faith. *Matthew 10:32-33, "Therefore whoever confesses me before men, him I will also confess before My Father who is in heaven" But whoever denies me before men, him I will also deny before My Father who is in heaven."* Baptism is an act of obedience that publicly declares one's faith. *Acts 2:37-38, "Now when they heard this, they were cut to the heart, and said to Peter and the rest of the apostles, "Men and brethren, what shall we do?"*

[38]Then Peter said to them, "Repent, and let every one of you be baptized in the name of Jesus Christ for the remission of sins; and you shall receive the gift of the Holy Spirit."

If you prayed that prayer and really meant it, I want to hear from you. Please write to me at the address on the back cover.

Before reading any further, let me explain the design of the following chapters. Each chapter and topic is designed to build a firm and solid foundation based on biblical principles. You need to take the information and scripture read in this chapter and ask God to build on it as you read the following chapter. This is why you see the words "Before continuing, have a moment of prayer." This request is so that, as you read each principle, you will allow the spirit of God to build into your life and mind these truths. The following chapters, with an earnest and sincere desire on your part, will build the foundation that will not crumble or be destroyed by this world or anything in it. Follow the steps in this book and God's Word and God Himself will guide you as you have started building on this new foundation in your life with Christ.

"BECAUSE OF LEE"
By R. Darryl Allgood

I have run so long, with my guilt and my shame,
The hurt in my heart, I cannot explain.
No dream or purpose have ever I known,
My life, my family, and all that I own.
All wasted and gone, dwindled away,
Not knowing the answer is all I can say.
A knock at my door one dark gloomy morn,
A child appeared, clothes withered and worn.
With a smile of contentment, happy with glee,
He gave me a tract and said "My name is Lee."
"Thank you," I said, as he went on his way,
He shouted, "He took it" on this one Christmas day.
I pondered a moment and thought for a while,
"Maybe this is it" as I spoke out loud.
I decided to read it, what have I to lose,
It's better to read, rather sit here and snooze.
A plan so warm, so loving, and kind,
I could not believe it was here all the time.
Transforming and wonderful it was all to me,
Simply because of a boy named Lee.
Years have passed since that wonderful day,
That little boy Lee has now passed away.
He yielded his life and obeyed a call,
Not knowing my life had reached a wall.
It is I now knocking from door to door,
Giving the plan to all rich and the poor.
I am very grateful for the willingness you see,
For I would not be here had it not been for Lee.

Take a few moments to reflect back on the truths and principles laid out in this chapter you have just completed. There may be decisions you have made that you don't want to forget. Reflecting on them, and implementing them, will help you set new goals and plan for achievements you desire to see in your life

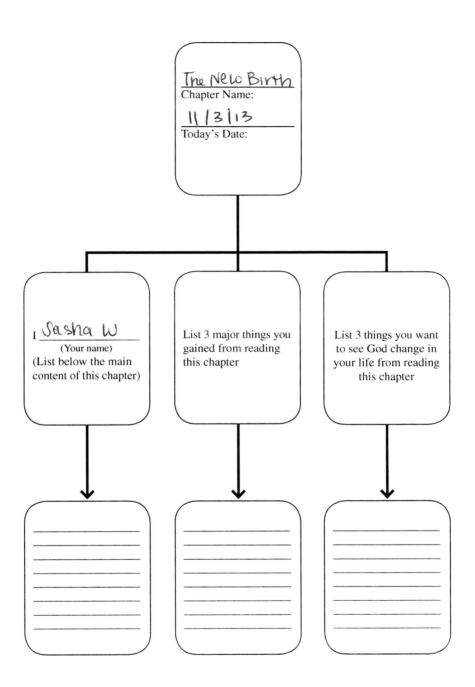

Chapter Name: The New Birth

Today's Date: 11/3/13

I Sasha W
(Your name)
(List below the main content of this chapter)

List 3 major things you gained from reading this chapter

List 3 things you want to see God change in your life from reading this chapter

13

CHAPTER 2

A NEW WALK

Romans 6:1-10

Chapter 2

A NEW WALK

(Before continuing, stop and have a moment of prayer.)

As I think back on our children when they were very small, I cannot help but remember when that most memorable stage arrived and they began to walk. Their eyes were so easily fascinated with the new objects and paths that they approached. Before you knew it, they would head in the direction that seemed the most intriguing. Then, as parents, we would quickly examine what was in their path to see if the direction was a good one or bad one. Our main concern was always whether the path they chose would lead to trouble or hurt. If the answer was positive, it would automatically put us into that mode of jumping to their defense. Redirection was always our final responsibility. In this chapter—"A New Walk"—you will see how similar the walk of a toddler is to the walk of a new Christian. Both have a very common nature.

Turn to and read the scripture referenced on the chapter title page before going any further. This passage is vitally important for understanding the new path and walk of life a young Christian pursues. The union you now have with Christ is one that will transform your walk for the rest of your life. In Romans, Paul is making us aware of the fact that we are no longer the same person we were before. Can you remember when a close family member or friend was killed or passed away? How did it make you feel over the next several weeks and months? If you are like me, it changed your outlook and gave you a new perspective on life for months and years to come. You were emotionally sensitive to everything you did and said, especially to those around you. In this passage of scripture, Paul is trying to convey that same message to you and me but in a behavioral and moral sense. He is focusing on the moral change of our physical life. In verse 1, Paul said *"Shall we continue in sin, that grace may abound?"* Paul was saying that we do not have a permit to continue to live that same way of life in sin as before, but that we are now changed in a newness of life. Therefore, we should have a new set of goals and ambitions to live toward. He then said *"God forbid. How shall we, that are dead to sin, live any longer in it?"* In other words, Paul was saying that we should now be walking in the direction opposite to where we were going before salvation. We are now walking and living a new walk.

The familiar draws us in to keep us where we are and where we have always been. It's like a magnet, drawing us to where it is comfortable and where we have the strongest ties. Since we have always known a certain way of life, it is easier to remain there. Go to and read *Exodus 13:1-5*. *"And Moses said unto the people, Remember this day, in which ye came out from Egypt, out of the house of bondage; for by strength of hand the LORD brought you out from this place: there shall no leavened bread be eaten. ⁴This day came ye out in the month Abib. ⁵And it shall be when the LORD shall bring thee into the land of the Canaanites, and the Hittites, and the Amorites, and the Hivites, and the Jebusites, which he sware unto thy fathers to give thee, a land flowing with milk and honey, that thou shalt keep this service in this month."*

God called their destination *"A land flowing with milk and honey."* But, in getting there, they will be challenged and stretched as never before. Keep this thought in mind; the children of Israel were brought out of situations, obstacles, troubles and bondage numerous times. This, of course, was God's promise to them and He never once let them down or went back on His promise. You ask the question, "What is to keep me from returning or falling back into the same old life I use to live and things I use to do on a daily manner?" Let me be the first to say that this question is one asked by many people each day. So, yes, it is a valid question. To answer your question, turn and read a little further in *Exodus 13:21-22:*²¹*And the LORD went before them by day in a pillar of a cloud, to lead them the way; and by night in a pillar of fire, to give them light; to go by day and night: ²²He took not away the pillar of the cloud by day, nor the pillar of fire by night, from before the people."* As God wanted His chosen people, the Israelites, freed from the bondage they were so engulfed in, He too, wants us to have that same freedom from our bondage today! He gave them the pillar of cloud and the fire to guide them and also to reassure them day and night that the destination was reachable. God gives us His word today as that same pillar that guides us and assures us that our destination is absolutely possible. I assure you that there will be unfamiliar surprises, unwanted fears, unpleasant adversaries, unfair accusations and unexpected resistance. It is always easier to stay on the known path where everything is business as usual. We must keep in mind that the untraveled path we have never known is where we will discover what the Lord has prepared for us.

In our New Walk as a Christian, strangeness alone is enough to tempt us to give up or go back to what we know; our old normal. We must recondition our body and our minds to prepare the proper reactions for what we encounter in our daily walk of life. In our physical body, we oftentimes must remap our body's movements. Our physical ability depends solely on the condition of our physical body. All of the muscles in our body work together in achieving actions like arm movement, finger and hand movement, and leg and foot bending. The timing of the movements of each muscle and tendon, in cooperation with the brain, is crucial, especially in actions like walking. What would happen if your left leg moved forward but the right leg and foot stayed still? You would take a nasty fall and hit the ground. The ability of our mind to properly sequence the movements of our legs and feet is a miracle of God's creation. In our Christian life, we also have a working together of our mind, soul and spirit. They, too, must be reconditioned as if we have had major surgery and are going through a recovery and rehabilitation process. You now are a changed vessel and have Christ living inside your heart and your life. To visually see life is one thing; but to handle life is a different story. The ability to successfully encounter life's trials, problems and difficulties comes from building character and firm principles into our life from the Word of God. You have a choice this very moment to accept the principles laid out in the Word of God and allow them to transform and be a part of your everyday being.

When a newborn child starts to crawl and then walk, we as parents must watch and guide them to make sure they stay in a safe area at all times. They are too young to understand the dangerous areas where they cannot go. This is why we constantly have them in our sight and care. In the *New Walk* as a Christian, we too, have to be aware of our surroundings. The next several steps are very important in your new walk with Christ.

❖ *Get to know the Word of God, the Bible.*
I Peter 2:2

Consider a classroom full of students. There, before the teacher, sit bundles of desire, if you will. Some of those desires within each child are wholesome, some mischievous, even bad. If the teacher sets out to primarily restrain the students' wayward desires, she will likely find herself in a nest of porcupines whose pricks of irritation will make her life miserable. The good teacher is one who dissolves the problems of discipline by arousing new interests. The effective principles in teaching, as in life, are to overcome the obstacles set before you and press on toward the goal. Picture, if you will, evil as darkness without light. The darkness cannot be driven out of a room with a fan or a sword but only by turning on the light. So; therefore, the evil or worldliness that is so prevalent around us each day must be banished with goodness. *1 John 1:7* said [7] *"But if we walk in the light, as he is in the light, we have fellowship with one another, and the blood of Jesus Christ his Son cleanseth us from all sin."*

As your New Walk begins as a Christian and child of God, it is very important that you start to read the Word of God on a daily basis. And this is the reason; God speaks and directs us through His word. In your New Walk, you must be aware of where you are going and what to expect along the way. The tremendous excitement you now possess, because of your salvation, naturally wants to overflow onto someone else. How can you be an effective tool in making that happen? The Word of God is the tool that we use to lead others to Christ. As you read it, you too will see how vitally important the work of the Holy Spirit is in bringing others to that same saving knowledge that you now cherish.

As a child, many years ago, I participated in an event in downtown Atlanta, Georgia where a clown was performing. I was not aware of cameras filming this event, and did not know it would be shown on television later that night. While we were at home resting, my mother had the television on watching the news. That very same clown came across the television screen. Well, wouldn't you know it, there I was standing right there beside the clown. My mother let out a joyful scream like you have never heard, simply because she was happy to see her son on television. I was excited too and wanted everyone to know that I was on television and to have a chance to see me; but the moment had happened and was gone. It was too late to spread the news so that others could see me as well. The news that eternal life is available to all, and that it is absolutely a free gift, is even more exciting than that. It is more exciting because it means eternity in heaven for you and me because someone has traded places with us, paying the price so that we will not have to spend an eternity in hell. This same reward is available to anyone and everyone if they will just believe and ask for it. This news is so exciting that we now want to know exactly how to tell someone else of that saving grace.

In *Ephesians 6:11*, Paul tells us that each day we live, we must put on the whole armor of God so that we may stand against the wiles of the devil. You have now changed sides in the battle and you now are a threat to Satan each time you share your testimony and the Word of God with others. You have the gospel of the Lord Jesus Christ and anyone you tell can accept this same free gift. This is why Paul said in *verse 12 "We wrestle not against flesh and blood, but against principalities, against powers and rulers of the darkness and spiritual wickedness in high places."* You now need, more than ever, to know exactly what God's word says and how to tell others of that same power and of that life-changing event.

The babies that are born into this world each day need milk to grow tall and strong, to fight off sickness and disease, and to make their bones good and strong. Just like babies need milk, we need the word of God to grow strong as a Christian. The Bible also states, in *1 Peter 2:2, "As newborn babes, desire the pure milk of the word that ye may grow by it."* In order to grow strong in the Lord Jesus Christ, we must have the nourishment that will only come from God's word.

A soldier in the military has to go through a basic training process. Why? Because he cannot go into war with no experience and no expectations of what is come. If he does, he will surely be killed. You and I must do the same sort of preparatory exercises in order to stand through the attack of the devil. The devil is slick and quick to deceive you and that is the exact reason we should know our enemy. In *II Timothy 2:15, it reads "Study to show thy self approved unto God, a workman that needeth not to be ashamed, rightly dividing the word of truth."* The ability to stand and know exactly what God's word tells us is a great ability. One who has this ability, stands in a very honorable position. Paul is telling us to study the Bible so that one day, when you or I stand in the presence of another; we can divide, or understand the scripture and what He has said. The one most important thing as a young Christian is that we read and learn the word of God.

Our heritage is very important to us. This is why some trace our family tree back years upon years, to see where it leads. Many people I know spend hours upon hours, days upon days, and even months upon months tracing back their lineage. As a child of God, I must do the same with the Word of God. This way, when old slew foot jumps up and tries to pull a slick one on you or me, the word of God that we have read and studied will be ready to defend and protect us. If Satan tried to pull a fast one on Jesus when he was praying in Gethsemane, he will pull the same move on you. The more you know, the stronger your foundation and the better prepared you are to fight him off.

As a new Christian, I suggest that you set a time each day, preferably the same time, and give that time to reading and studying the word of God. If you predetermine and fix this time, you will be more likely to protect this time that you have given to God. This is your daily source of strength and power and is more important than any other. This time must be set in stone or you will find other things taking over and you will not do it. It may take a little time, but remember this; anything that is done 27 times in a row will become a habit. Hebrews 11:6 states that God will reward and bless them that diligently seek Him.

Can you remember a time in school when everyone was to read a book by a certain date and then discuss it? When it came time for the discussion, remember how good it felt to know what everyone was talking about? This is the exact same thing when it comes to the word of God. Also, just as we would want to know the person that pulled us from a burning building and saved our life, we will want to know all we can about our Savior.

❖ *Get involved in a Good Bible-believing Church.*
Hebrews 10:25

The Bible instructs us to be part of a local church and tells us the purpose of doing so. *"Not forsaking the assembling of ourselves together, as is the manner of some, but exhorting one another, and so much the more as you see the day approaching."* The greatest tragedy among many young Christians is that they do not get involved with other Christians. Our spiritual growth hinges on our involvement in a good local church. You may visit several churches at first but, ultimately, you need to be involved in a local Church. I will never forget the lady that visited our Sunday school class for the first time. These were her exact words, "I never thought this could be such a good experience and also fun." The

Church program will place you in contact with people your age, some of whom may be in very similar circumstances. This is vitally important to your growth. Other young Christians can be a help to you and can also be friends that understand the same life issues that you are encountering. The fellowship of other Christians will strengthen your bond as well as give you a Christian family.

Have you ever watched the manufacturing of a rope? It begins as one strand of string and then is wound with another and another until it becomes one or more inches thick. Do you know how strong that rope has now become? It is much stronger than the single string and, because of the way it is wound; it is even stronger than the simple combination of several strings. That is what your involvement in Sunday school and church will do for you and your family. We cannot survive without it. You may say, "I just can't meet people" or "I am not good at talking to new people." That is perfectly OK, and I know exactly what you mean, but you do not have to speak any more than five words. All you have to say is, "My name is _____ _____." That's it. The rest will fall right into place.

In a typical conversation, they will respond, "I am Mary or Joe"; they will then tell you where they are from and whether they have children. They will say they have been members of that church for a certain number of months or years. After this simple start and conversation, you will have made a new friend and you may find yourself wishing you had done this even sooner. The good feelings that come from just knowing other people are feelings like no other. Imagine a large room of people and everyone are strangers. They all may feel uneasy and nervous until one person stands and tells another his name and where he is from. Then another person stands and does the same. What will eventually happen? No one will be a stranger any longer. It is just as simple as saying, "My name is Darryl Allgood."

I will never forget the night I was in Atlanta, Georgia at the age of eighteen and we were at our high school prom. As I was standing in the hotel lobby, a man walked up to me and reached out his hand and said "Hi there, I am Ronald Reagan and I am running for president." I did not even know the man was a movie star, much less running for the office of President of the United States of America. You ask me "Were you nervous?" My answer is "No, I was not" because I did not know this man and he did not know me. We were strangers and all it took was a handshake and an introduction. Our relationships start with a small spark and, before you know it, you have a huge family. This family will include departments for babies, children, teenagers, young adults and groups going all the way up to senior citizens. There cannot be any more happiness than there is with a Church Family that cares when you're sad, when you have lost a family member or friend, when you are hospitalized or dealing with any other event in your life. This family is there for you and for me. That is why I use the example of the strength of the rope.

❖ *Inquire and Attend a Sunday School Program:*

In the previous section, I referred to the different departments in the church, from the nursery all the way up to the senior citizen's program. I mentioned that for a very important reason. You and I fall into one of those categories, no matter who you may be. The Sunday School program is one of the best parts of the church. I fondly remember the times I taught children's church some years ago. A little girl by the name of Melissa came up to me and she was only eight years old. As I would sing songs and tell Bible stories to those children, I was helping to mold their lives into adulthood. Today, many years later, I see this same girl and she has her own family including children of her own. She was part of a program that helped her prepare for the day that would come when she would use those things learned in Sunday school to teach her own children.

Regardless of age or station in life, a Sunday School program helps you study and learn the word of God and builds bonds between you and other Christians There is a couple who mean the world to us and are our dearest friends simply because of the time we share in church and Sunday school. When my wife's mother passed away, this couple immediately came to our home with food and comfort. This couple became our friends solely through our church and Sunday School program. I do not know what we would do without them. God allowed us to meet this couple simply because He knew we would need them one day, as they have needed us. It has created a bond with friends that cannot come from any other source. The Sunday School program reinforces Bible principles that help us today and prepare us for days and months to come. How many places can you go where you feel safe and protected in a family atmosphere? The Sunday School program is designed to be a clean, safe and learning environment for all ages. You can participate without the fear of vulgar language or obscene gestures. The church activities that are planned are designed to build up and encourage every person, no matter who they may be.

Another area of real importance in church and Sunday School is the pastor. There may be times when we will get confused or need to sit and talk with someone about very personal issues. The pastor and his wife are trained and experienced in this area specifically. There is no greater comfort than to be in a critical position and have one to lean on for comfort and direction. It does not matter what time of the day or night, your pastor will care for you and your family and he will come to your aide. The Bible describes him as a shepherd and he looks out for and cares for his sheep. Imagine a shepherd boy in the field. As he counts his flock, he notices one is hurt or one is missing. He will leave his entire flock to go and rescue that one sheep. That is the same compassion a pastor shows for the ones who are a part of the church. These are benefits that come from being involved, and they are countless.

❖ *Set Regular Times to Pray:*

Prayer and faith go hand in hand. If you have no faith, then there will be no prayers. A life of prayer can only exist as long as you have faith. Jesus told Peter to be careful because Satan desired to sift him as wheat. Jesus was telling Peter to guard his faith and not let his guard down. If your faith is gone, stolen or dwindled away, you have nothing. Your spiritual growth must have a solid base and the true foundation of your prayer life is built upon your faith. *Philippians 4:6, "Be anxious for nothing, but in everything by prayer and supplication, with thanksgiving, let your requests be made known to God;"*

Our faith is displayed when we truly pray. Why does God want us to pray? Doesn't he already know what we are in need of and doesn't he want us to have those things? Yes, He does, but prayer is our way of starting a conversation with God.

I remember when one of my grandchildren came to me and said, "Pepaw, can I have some of that ice cream in the freezer?" I would respond to him, "Why do you want some ice cream?" He would say, "Because it is good and I would like to have some." I then would say, "But why?" He responded, "Because you are the best Pepaw in the whole wide world." After a time of getting all these compliments, what do you think I did? You are correct; I gave him the ice cream. God is like that also. He wants to give us things but He wants us to talk to Him and tell Him how great He is. Then, at the proper time, place, and circumstance, He will answer our prayers. We too, show our faith when we pray and ask God to direct us, comfort us and give us peace. A chair with four legs that is placed against the wall is a good and secure seat. However, You and I cannot know this personally until we choose to actually sit down and place 100% of our trust in that chair. Our faith in God is the same way. We must realize that, without prayer, there is no faith. Only God can move mountains, but faith and prayer can actually move God. *Mark 11:24 "Therefore I say unto you, whatever things ye desire, when you pray, believe that ye receive them and ye shall have them."* Prayer also enables the mind of God to be in you. *Philippians 2:5, "Let this mind be in you which was also in Christ Jesus,"*

Our communication with God reveals to Him our earnest desire to do what's right and follow Him where He may lead us. After kneeling in earnest prayer, we arise with peace in our soul and love in our heart that will continue to exist no matter what comes our way. We can rely on His promise given in *I Corinthians 10:13, "There hath no temptation taken you but such as is common to man; but God is faithful, who will not permit you to be tempted above that ye are able, but will, with the temptation, also make the way to escape, that ye may be able to bear it."* We are furnished with the Holy Spirit at the time of our salvation, to enable us to conquer whatever comes our way. You and I each will encounter temptations all through our life; it is natural, but that does not mean we have to give in. The Bible teaches us to resist the devil and he shall flee from us. Prayer is where you gain the majority of the strength you need to overcome your battles. As you arise each morning, you must feed your body in order to start your day. Not eating will, in turn, cause a lack of energy, which will eventually cause a breakdown. Prayer is a necessity just as food is.

Faith is the foundation of Christian character. As the days, months and years go by, man becomes more and more self-dependant. I will never forget September 11, 2001 when the twin towers in New York were attacked by two hijacked commercial aircraft. As the United States of America had never known anything of this nature, our president, this country's leader, sought prayer like never before. And the people of the USA responded, as churches were filled and people joined together in prayer and action. It is now 2012, eleven years later, and this country has forgotten what prayer can and will do for this land. Man is becoming colder and colder toward the things of God and faith in God. The more we as Christians pray, the stronger our faith in and dependence on God will become.

To advance as we should in a Christian's journey, we must learn early on the importance of the moral life; we must surely grasp the serious meanings of right and wrong. Take time now and read *II Peter 1:1-14* before you go any further. Peter tells us of great Christian character and virtues we need in our life in order to succeed. Peter tells us how we can live with fruitfulness and security. He said *"Grace and peace be multiplied unto you through the knowledge of God and of Jesus, our Lord."* In order for grace and our peace to be even greater, we must read God's word daily which, in turn, enhances our knowledge of the word of God. This actually confirms our need to read and meditate on God's word. Peter then said, *"By which are given unto us exceeding great and precious promises, that by these ye might be partakers of the divine nature, having escaped the corruption that is in the world through lust."* Our Christian growth should be as a group of trained musicians, such as Heman or Asaph in the days of David and Solomon. As each instrument plays in tune with the others, it creates the most balanced sound you have ever heard. Our life must be just as balanced in order to overcome the battles and potholes we will encounter and go through.

Our life as Christians has a path and direction that will cause us to face many obstacles. As we look at a mountain on a fresh and early morning, we see the glittering of the dew on the trees from the sun as it rises above the top of the mountain. How beautiful and glorious it is to view God's unique handiwork. Our life travels a path that takes us near to mountains in our lives. We look at this mountain and see sharp and ragged edges, slick and dangerous spots along the way. It has deep gullies, where water flows in swift currents after the rain and unsheltered platforms. We have all faced this mountain at one point or another.

As we stop to pray each day, we see more and more the impact of God's grace as it grows into a larger portion of our life. It only comes from daily prayer. Faith and prayer are the great virtues that will make men and women great for God. Your goal should be to start praying and build into your life this time alone with God no matter what. You are building a structured aspect in your life that will not fall or cave in. Your existence as a strong Christian one year, two years, three years, and five years from now depends on that time in prayer. *"Be careful for nothing but in everything by supplication and prayer, with thanksgiving, let your requests be made known unto God. "Philippians 4:6.*

"BABIES DON'T QUIT"
By RD Allgood

A small child, growing up in stages, has never known fear or being afraid as he attempts new things each day of his life. I can remember when my first child was taken to his grandparents at his crawling and slowly walking stage. He would hold to the coffee table and work his way around it, touching and even trying to pick up things he had never seen before. When he turned loose of the table and attempted to walk away, he would fall and roll over, but would get back on his knees and work his way back to the coffee table and try it again and again. He finally was able to walk away from the table with more stability and strength than he had before.

Now, he is in his early twenties and a senior in college. Years have passed since he was that small and I know, as a parent, we all can agree to similar stories as this. There is another area of these stories we tend to overlook. Our lives as young or older adults can be halted due to a trial or tragedy that has arrived in our path. We attempt to face it with strength, but with our strength and not God's. We approach the table as the small child does and when we turn loose, we do well for a second or two, but we then tumble and fall down and begin to worry, fret and then realize, "Hey, let's try it again." This time, we attempt it with more caution and a better understanding of what is needed to make it work with more and added strength. This comes with time and practice, not forgetting patience and endurance. I like the old saying by Timex Watches, "They take a licking and keep on ticking." That philosophy can be adopted by each of us as well. The life we live will always have obstacles, bumps and even potholes, but that is ok and acceptable as long as we remember this one thought—even though we fall, face a major crisis or some other event, we can get up, make up our mind as that child did and go full speed ahead. It's ok that we fall or stumble along the way; this is our learning process which, in return, will bring us wisdom. Therefore, we too are the babies that don't quit.

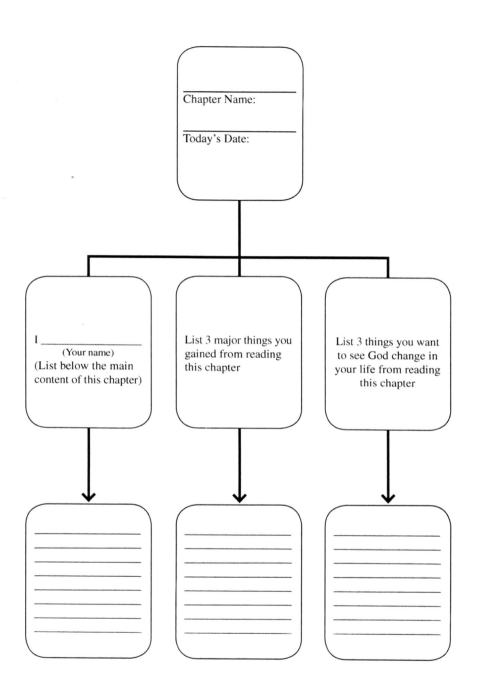

Chapter Name:

Today's Date:

I _____
(Your name)
(List below the main
content of this chapter)

List 3 major things you
gained from reading
this chapter

List 3 things you want
to see God change in
your life from reading
this chapter

CHAPTER 3

THE BUILDING OF NEW TRUTHS

Matthew 7:24-27

Chapter 3

THE BUILDING OF NEW TRUTHS

(Before continuing, stop and have a moment of prayer.)

This chapter will reveal the truths that will help you build a solid biblical foundation into your life and strengthen your walk as a new or young Christian. The Bible tells us in *Matthew 7:24-27 "the wise man built his house upon the rock and the foolish man upon the sand and when the storms and winds came, only the house built upon the rock and solid foundation withstood the weather."* This principle is the one to be used in beginning and stabilizing many areas of our life. By accepting Christ as your Savior, you have laid the most important stone. You now are a young Christian with a foundation for building all biblical principles upon. This first step leads you to the building stages of laying truths into your life that will carry you through storms today and for years and decades to come. This is what I call a set of new truths instilled in one's life. All the years before now, you have relied on things that seemed normal and routine. Now, you are using God and His Word to build something that will last throughout eternity.

Take a look at a brick wall. It takes many single bricks to get a full wall of protection and stability built. In our illustration, each brick is a symbol of a biblical truth. The more bricks you lay, the stronger and taller your wall becomes. As you will see, the arrows of life will be hurled at us but the principles we build today will secure our life and deflect these enemies and their attacks. The benefits of the wall will allow you to continue to stand and to stand strong.

The process of building a set of new and solid truths into your life will enable your life to become substantially stout and strong. You will build a life that will stand through storms and situations in life that may otherwise cause you to collapse or retreat.

If you will allow this section into your daily life and walk, I promise that you will see a transformation in your days, months and years to come. Do not just read these principles, but allow them to become a part of your daily life. Take index cards, write a biblical truth on each, and place them on your bathroom mirror, nightstand, refrigerator door or coffee pot. Each time you see them, you are reminding and teaching yourself a vital truth of God. By instilling these truths into your life, you are programming your response to specific situations. By programming your response, you have won 99% of the battle. Then you will be at work one day and a situation will arise. Because you have this truth instilled in your life, you will be ready to defeat the devil and claim the victory through your knowledge of the truths of God.

❖ *First Truth: God's Promise*

A promise is the assurance that one will do a particular thing or that guarantees that a particular thing will happen. God's promises are very real and true, no matter how we may feel at any given time. You cannot base your salvation on how you feel. We must base it on God's truth and that truth is the Word of God. We may feel saved in today's sunny weather, but tomorrow may be rainy and full of storms. Our feelings change from one day to the next, but truth never changes. *Malachi 3:6.* God said, *"I am the Lord, I change not . . ."* God's promises will always prove true and everlasting. You can always depend on them no matter what may come your way. We know that feelings are good and bad at times, so this is all the more reason to build something solid that we can rely on. *John 14:6, "Jesus said unto him, I am the way, the truth and the life, no man cometh to the father but by me."* Jesus was speaking to His apostles and comforting them with the promise of His returning. To have this truth that God is returning to take his children home is a promise that is well worth working and waiting for.

God's word gives us general and also specific promises. You and I build our lives on the general promises such as *1 John 1:9* where John was describing the fellowship we have with God as He promises *"If we confess our sin, He is faithful and just to forgive us our sins and cleanse us from all unrighteousness."* This is the nature and truth of God and it is available to any man, woman, boy or girl.

The story of a father and son depicts this truth very well. Bobby had been instructed by his dad not to ride his bicycle near the main road and, of course, it was for a good reason. One day after school, Bobby came home and began to ride the bicycle near the end of the street. As he was riding, he did not realize how close he had gotten to the corner and, before you know it, the boy was on the main road. A truck driver coming down the road saw the boy just in the nick of time and laid on his horn. The boy was so frightened; he jumped from the bicycle and rolled to the side of the street. The truck could not help but destroy the boys bicycle. Bobby was so frightened that his dad would not forgive him that he went home and sat in his room and began to weep. When his dad arrived home, he rushed to his son to make sure he was ok. As the dad looked down at his son, this is what he said, "Son, I felt helpless as I was so far away from you and could not help you to safety. I instilled in you a truth to stay away from the main road and as long as you would stay away from the main road, you had the promise of protection." Bobby's dad then said, "You knew what that truth was and now you know why that truth was so important. You are my son and always will be and the love I have for you allows me to instill truths into your life to build and protect you. Your safety is very important to me and I want nothing to ever harm you." They embraced for over forty-five minutes because a truth had become reality.

God's love and promise is even greater because His love is unconditional and has no limits. *Philippians 4:8-9* also teaches us to do the things that are true, honest, just and pure. These things can be instilled in us and our families and God's promise is the reward of peace. Have you ever told a lie about something and felt really bad? That night, as you tried to rest and go to sleep, your conscience would not allow you. That comes from knowing right from wrong. God rewards us with the promise of a peaceful mind when we pursue these things. God also wants us to leave our every care on Him. When the little boy above finally realized that dad was teaching him in order to protect him from harm arid misery, the boy knew real and compassionate love. The promises below are just some of God's many promises and truths:

> Promises when you are deserted by loved ones: Psalms 9:10; 27:10; I Peter 5.7
> Promises when you are in financial trouble: Psalms 23; 34:10; Luke 6:38
> Promises when you are in grief: I Thessalonians 4:13; II Thessalonians 2:16
> Promises when you are waiting on God: Psalms 27:14; 33:20; Hebrews 10:23

Mark 3:10b

Promises when you do not understand God's ways: Isaiah 55:8; I Cor. 10:13

Promises when you are discouraged: Psalms 138. 7; Phil. 4:6-8; I Peter 1. 6-9

Promises of God in Psalms: 4:3; 5:12; 15:2; 23;

Promises when you feel tempted: Romans 6:14; I Cor. 10:12-13; Heb. 4:14-16

Promises when you are lonely: Matt. 28:20; John 14:1, 18.

Promises when you feel confused: I Cor. 14:33, II Tim. 1:7; I Peter 4:12-13

❖ *Second Truth: God's Grace*

The word *grace* means undeserved acceptance and love received from another. God's grace was bestowed upon us even when we were not yet born. In the truth of grace, God's love and care for us is real and true. *Matthew 11:28: "Come unto me, all ye that labor and are heavy laden, and I will give you rest."* The amount of grace that it takes to include *"all"* is immeasurable. The ultimate fact is this: without grace we are doomed; we are hopelessly lost with no chance of being saved. *John 1:17* tells us that *"Grace and Truth came by Jesus Christ"* and because of this, we can be saved for eternity. The word grace in the New Testament comes from a Greek word *"charis"*. It is used approximately 150 times in the New Testament alone. I tell you this because, without the truth of grace in our lives, we would be destined for eternal death. When Jesus came to die for you and me, though He knew no sin, grace abounded even that much more. *John 3:18* tells us *"He that believeth on Him (Jesus, the son of God) is not condemned; but he that believeth not is condemned already, because he hath not believed in the name of the only begotten Son of God."* The condemnation has been removed from the one who has accepted Jesus as their Savior, and that my friend, is true GRACE. God's grace is abundant and it never runs out. The amount of God' grace is always greater than the depth of our sin. The apostle Paul described it best this way; *Romans 5:20, "God's grace multiplied where sin increased"*. When you think back to the day Jesus was placed on that wooden cross, what do you see? Imagine standing on the sideline of a crowd as the guards prepare the nails that will soon pierce His hands and feet. What do you feel? This man will soon die a physical death, suffering both physical and spiritual pain that we cannot even imagine. And He suffered this penalty in payment for what others had done, not for anything that He had done. When I stop and remember this, I cannot keep from weeping because I do not deserve such a gift. When you think of grace, what comes to your mind? How do you define your life when you think of Grace?

❖ *Third Truth: God's Strength*

When we go to court, we swear to tell the truth, and nothing but the truth. The entire judicial process is based on a foundation of truth. This is only reasonable, since we know that anything worth building must be built on a solid foundation.

The truth, biblical truth, becomes the strength in all we do. God's strength is made perfect in our weakness. It is in the moments of our worst and lowest times that God's image is seen most clearly in our lives. This at times can be a painful process. Imagine back God sending His son to this earth and then seeing Him crucified on a cross at Calvary. Yet, this was the time and place that humanity was born into the family of God. It is weakness in us that allows God to shine and display His wondrous power and grace. God's strength is immeasurable. In order to personally know this strength, you must first witness it within your own life.

Anyone can tell you a boat will carry you over to the other side of the lake, but unless you have been in that boat, you really don't know how far it will carry you. I can reassure you of all God's promises and assure you they are true, but unless you actually come to rely on God's word, you will never truly know that sweet assurance and peace. The word of God is designed to give the child of God direction and assurance in every aspect of his or her life. Have you ever been in a town you did not know or have you ever tried to find your way home without a map? Do you remember becoming frustrated and maybe even afraid that you were lost? Did you feel very strong or very weak? Like most people, you probably felt weak because you were lost. Now, let's say you had a map and the directions were as plain as day. You can now make it home in a very short time with no threat of danger or possibility of ending getting lost. God's word has the same design, it is a roadmap for our lives, and all we have to do is rely on it.

Another way we can see God's strength is to look at how he made each person different and with unique personalities. That requires the ultimate ability to make people similarly human but with so many different characteristics. His sovereignty is so amazing that I cannot even begin to describe it. How do you describe one that is so strong and yet so lovingly compassionate? Take a few minutes and list ten to fifteen ways you would describe God's strength. After you have done this, ask yourself this question: If God is this strong, why do I not trust him more each day? There is an old gospel song wrote by John H. Sammis in 1887 by the name "Trust And Obey" that goes like this:

When we walk with the Lord, in the light of his word,
What a glory he sheds on our way.
While we do his good will, he abides with us still,
and with all who will trust and obey.

The message is that there is strength along with comfort in obeying and walking with God. So after reading this section, you can only conclude that real strength is with God, which leads us to simply Trusting God.

❖ *Fourth Truth: Trusting God*

I was reading a while back about how we react to adversity and how troubling it is to hear of so many cases of cancer, rebellious teenagers, companies going under due to financial difficulties, the loss of a baby in the course of a pregnancy, the despair of a young parent who has just learned of a terminal illness and many other problems that are encountered all across this land. As I sat and considered this, I could not help but quote *1 John 4:4, "Greater is he that is in me than he that is in the world."* This is a faithful truth that I have instilled inside of me knowing that adversities will come no matter who we are or how old we may be. So I have learned to just trust God.

By trusting God, you are saying *"It is in His hands."* Does this ability come easily? No it does not because we are human and it is very difficult and even painful at times. It only comes from the placing of and building upon these biblical truths in one's life. These truths will intertwine with all that we do and say. It should be what makes our life worth living even more. I can remember the day when I surrendered to God and committed to Him every aspect of my life. I began to change the way I viewed all aspects of life and its adversities. My days were given to Him every morning, no matter what may come.

On one particular day after I had given my life to God, I encountered an event just the thought of which makes many people shiver and seek to avoid. A senior manager called me into the office at the company where I was employed. He had the duty of laying me off from my job due to the downsizing of the company. I was shocked and yet prepared because I had instilled the truths of God within my mind and within my heart. I trusted God 100%, no matter what. There is a verse that will give you comfort and direction no matter what the storm may drag into your life. God's word is one huge promise just as *I Peter 3:12* said, *"For the eyes of the Lord are over the righteous, and His ears are open unto their prayers."* God's ability to be over His children and hear their every prayer is a promise he gave to each of us. Trusting God must have a starting point in order to begin to sprout and grow.

We all can expect to experience emotional stress and anxieties in our life. But, keep in mind, it is through the working out of these adversities that life is brought forth and we encounter growth in God. As for God's people, it seems we experience this more than the unbeliever. Why is that? Why does it seem that God sits on the throne in Heaven instead of rescuing his children? Let's go back to the day when Jesus was in the garden praying to God the Father before his death on Calvary. He said in *Mark 22:42, "Father, if thou be willing, remove this cup from me; nevertheless, not my will, but thine be done."* Jesus knew that, in order to bring forth abundant life, his death was necessary. Did Jesus want to die in torment like this? What do you think? I believe that Jesus, the son of God, never, ever knew pain or torture like He was about to suffer. Yet, knowing what was in store for Him, He was still fully willing to trust God and suffer the pain of retribution for all sin on our behalf. The ability to trust God comes by looking all the way through our circumstances and setting our eyes upon the victory on the other side of our adversity. Each positive and faithful step we take, or each anxiety and adversary we face, our nurturing and growth becomes stronger and deeper rooted.

Think of the old oak tree that grows by the river with roots that go so deep. It is almost impossible to blow it over. Daily positive living with assurance only comes by trusting God. *Proverbs 27:1* said, *". . . for thou knowest not what a day may bring forth."* As I lay my head down to sleep at night, the roots of those truths lie deep down in my soul and I trust God for the next day. We cannot live tomorrow on the strength God has given us today, it is impossible. You and I can worry, fret and even come unglued about tomorrow but guess what? It will not change a thing at all other than give us grey hair, ulcers, strokes and heart attacks. All of our worry will be in vain because God is the only one that holds tomorrow in the palm of His hand. I choose to take God's hand and rest tonight, and take on tomorrow when tomorrow gets here.

I wrote the poem below several years back and it portrays exactly what we are learning each day, no matter who we may be. The ability to draw true strength and trust come from this principle.

"PERFECT STRENGTH"

By R. Darryl Allgood

People say that they can make it; they rely upon their strength,
No need for Bible direction, they're strong though never weak.
But then a sudden crash, as life drops to the ground,
Thinking all is lost and over, pondering on heaven bound.
You say you're satisfied but thoughts of fear await,
And when you think of death, you ask "What is my fate?"
Oh real and perfect strength is always found with Him,
No worries about tomorrow, His light is never dim.
Just when I think it's over, He always shows His face,
Giving me another day, filled with love and tender grace.
Now you think of all your friends, family members too,
And wonder how you can tell them, what Christ has done for you.
Just stop and count your blessings, name them one by one,
It surely will amaze them, what God has daily done.
Now strength, it is not purchased or requires a certain class,
Just simply come to Jesus, which is all the Savior asks.
Oh real and perfect strength, is always found with Him,
No worries about tomorrow, His light is never dim.
Just when I think it's over, He always shows His face-
Giving me another day, filled with love and tender grace.

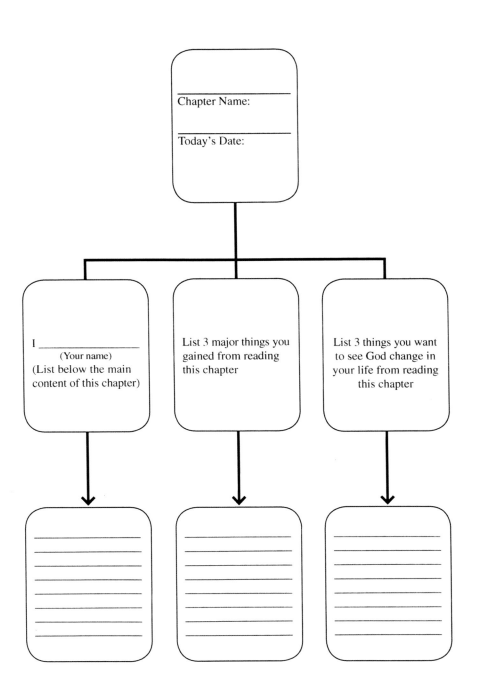

Chapter Name: _____

Today's Date: _____

I _____
(Your name)
(List below the main content of this chapter)

List 3 major things you gained from reading this chapter

List 3 things you want to see God change in your life from reading this chapter

CHAPTER 4

YOU'RE A NEW LIFE

II Corinthians 5:17

Chapter 4

YOU'RE A NEW LIFE

(Before continuing, stop and have a moment of prayer.)

What is the true meaning of life? What was I born for and why? *II Corinthians 5:17, "¹⁷ Therefore, if anyone is in Christ, he is a new creation; old things have passed away; behold, all things have become new."* You now have a new life that is accompanied by a wonderful and tremendous knowledge that, as a Christian, this new life will last for eternity. Also, keep in mind that the new life you have not only comes with joy and excitement but it also comes with a new title. *Titus 3:7, "that having been justified by His (God's) grace we should become heirs according to the hope of eternal life."* You are now an heir of God, which entitles you to the blessings and riches that come with being an heir. Remember the earlier illustration regarding the man that was upset about his obituary notice? That is the example to keep in mind as an illustration of a new life as well as a new birth.

The realization that God has given you a new life may result in discomfort when we think about all the things that were done before becoming a Christian. Always remember that people are human, will remember you as you were and will watch to see what changes are taking place in our lives. Keep in mind that we are sinners saved by Grace. Someone will always be there to question us or remind us about what we were and did before we were saved. That's ok, and should be unexpected. Our past is the past and our new life and new road we now travel is one that will still have potholes. But now we have the "whole armor of God" that gives us the tools and equipment we need to defeat those obstacles. This means that, as Christ has saved you and enriched your ability to live led by the Holy Spirit, you are now a New Life with God as the center from this point forward. *Romans 8:6 said, "For to be carnally minded is death, but to be spiritually minded is life and peace."*

When a person receives a promotion at their place of employment, it usually includes a new title. When I was a supervisor, I had responsibilities that I was to perform each day. When I was promoted to production manager, my responsibilities grew as well. I was rewarded as a supervisor but, when I took on the new position, I received even greater rewards. The new job increased in duties and responsibilities and required greater performance. It is a blessing and honor to achieve a promotion, but it also brings on a new realm of daily activities.

Taking part in something great is talked about for years and decades. Think about the first light bulb and how Thomas A. Edison must have felt knowing that he had a part in history in the making. That was something great back then. Similarly, you are part of something even greater today. You are on your way to heaven! You are a new life and that life has the ability to impact others and make eternal history.

The gift that God provides comes to us with this price; the death of His son on the cross of Calvary. Imagine that you are blind and that you are walking straight out into traffic. A man stops you just in time and points you in a new direction that will be safe and not life-threatening. How would you feel as you walk in this new direction?

I personally walked with a skip of delight each step of the way versus just a regular walk. *"Therefore, if any man is in Christ, he is a new creation; old things are passed away; behold, all things are become new."* That day, the day I came to know Jesus as my Savior, was when I truly started living a peaceful and joyful life. I was able to see my life for what it truly was. Those times of drinking it up, partying all night and running off with a wild group was not a joy any longer. I became a new creation in God and it transformed the way I saw and thought about all the things around me. When you accepted Christ, that day started a whole new life for you as well. Your old ways and desires should now change because you are going in a new direction with new goals and ambitions. You must accept today for what it is and also accept the fact you can only be what you are by the grace of God. You are a new life in Christ and can lean on Him to stand up to others who want to change who and what you are. I remember a man that was an alcoholic, but God saved him. He had the ability to work on cars and was a tremendous mechanic. Does the fact that one is an alcoholic prevent the use of the talents God gives? No. The past afflictions can become sources of strength and increase our current abilities. A man from the bottle became the best mechanic in town. God will allow the past to become stepping stones of success in the future.

❖ *The Need to Set New Goals:*
Philippians 3:10-19

You are now a new life no matter what may be in the past. You have a brand new start in Christ Jesus. In verse 13, Paul said, "*. . . this one thing I do, forgetting those things which are behind, and reaching forth unto those things which are before,*" He is telling us to first, forget about where we have been up to this point. The past is the past. From now on, reach forward and set new goals in your life. For an example, a person I know used to be an alcoholic. Then God saved them and they have been sober for 14 months. I praise the Lord they are sober today. This person has set out to learn accounting and be more responsible than ever before. They are aiming at running for City Council in the next five to ten years. That is an example of what can take place in your life. His ultimate goal is to be a professing Christian City Councilman and, in turn, to be a witness to God's ability to transform a person's life to others in the community. In verse 14, he said "*I press toward the mark for the prize of the high calling of God in Christ Jesus.*" Paul said to push yourself, strive and reach toward your aspirations in accomplishing new goals in your life. Paul compared it to a prize. I know what it feels like to win a prize, do you? It is a great feeling to have. In the same way, that you reached your goal is a great accomplishment.

In the humanistic world we live in, people pursue many purposes, thinking they will eventually find the ultimate meaning in life. Some people pursue business success, doing good for others, wealth, a good and successful family, and expensive luxuries. Even when they reach their goals, an empty feeling or deep void inside still exists and cannot be filled without Christ. People have testified that, even after achieving their loftiest goals, they were still unhappy. I remember reading an article a while back where a baseball player had played for years, striving to reach the top. After he had been inducted into the Hall of Fame, a reporter asked, "What is it you wish someone would have told you years ago when you first started playing ball?" The player thought before responding and then said this, "I wish someone would have told me that when you reach the top, there is nothing there." The many goals people achieve every day are filled with emptiness, but they never find out until it is way too late. The greatest enemy in the setting of goals is the lack of a plan. Many people set out to be successful at one thing

Col. 6:4
church announce
there

or another, but the lack of a plan, and working that plan regularly, destroys the possibility of reaching the goal from the beginning. There are three aspects to successfully setting and reaching a goal: (1) setting an achievable goal; (2) planning for what it will take to get there and (3) setting miniature goals along the way to move you toward the major goal.

Let's say I want to take my family to Hawaii for a week. Do I wait until the day before I leave to plan or do I lay out a succession of small steps to achieve that major goal of the actual trip? To achieve the trip successfully, we will lay out the mini goals and will arrive at Hawaii more quickly. The goal is to go to Hawaii and the plan is what I need in order to get from here to there. The steps in the plan include the date we are leaving, which airline we will use, where we will stay, how much money we will need, which clothes we will need and what we will do. All of these actions are objectives and once they are all accomplished, the goal will be met. Each objective may have several action steps in order for that objective to be completed.

In your new life as a Christian, you must take time to set new goals for your life as well as for your family. What you do and how you do it is being measured each and every day. What are your goals to meet by the end of this month? Do you have any? If not, you will not get very far. What are your goals to meet by the end of this year? Some people say to make more money, to quit certain habits, to live healthier. Whatever that goal may be, you must set objectives to meet at a minimum of every three months in order to achieve that larger goal. The same principle applies in your Christian life goal-setting. Reading the Bible through in a year can be broken down to some number of verses and chapters a day. If you follow your plan, in six months you are halfway to your yearly goal. As you set goals, set them personally and also set them for your family. Make sure they are reachable and not way too high. You want to inspire yourself by setting goals you have to stretch for but can still reach. It is so easy to get carried away in setting a goal and set it too high. When we fail to reach a goal, we may become discouraged and too hard on ourselves for not getting there. That will bring unwanted discouragement and we often fail to try it again. We set ourselves up to fail because we were not wise enough in setting a practical goal.

The most rewarding feeling we can give ourselves is the feeling of achievement. No matter who you are or what you set out to accomplish, when you achieve it, you will feel like you are sitting on top of the world. You used wisdom to set the goal and develop the plan, and then you did what you said you would do. That is ACHIEVEMENT. You should celebrate or treat yourself to something special, right? It can be just a milk shake or a new dress or a new tie. The fact is that you accomplished what you set out to do and that is a great feeling. In your Christian life, the devil has many traps set up to make you stumble along the way. That is to be expected because we know that is the way he works. What you and I must do is preset goals to avoid his traps and obstacles. When you set a goal to defeat the devil this year, your objectives may be to read your Bible daily, pray for thirty minutes daily, and memorize two verses of scripture weekly. The goal of more victories has now been preset and predetermined by your objectives. When Satan tries to defeat us and make us fall, we will have a foundation that cannot be shaken. We have set Christian goals that will in turn build Christian character in our life. You are building a defense system that will deflect the enemy's darts. You must set goals like these to have that solid foundation that will not crumble or fall.

❖ *Have Great Ambitions:*
Philippians 4:13 & 19

We now know how vitally important the setting of new goals is in our life, but we must also have the fuel needed to propel us forward. Some people may say they aim to become the president of the United States of America, or they have the goal of becoming the greatest scientist to ever live, or maybe they want to be the most famous person in the world of engineering. Whatever the ambition may be, you must ultimately ask yourself this question, "What will be the end result of meeting all the goals and ambitions set in my life?" Ambition is the fuel that moves us from the starting line all the way to the goal or achievement. You must first have a goal and then draw out your detailed plan to reach the goal. This is difficult for many to grasp, but the desire to be a great achiever is only part of the task. To be an ambitious person is a very good sign because, with ambitions, a person strives to achieve greatness. Some have huge ambitions, some large and many have very small ambitions. Why is that? Why do so many people have such limited ambitions?

Ambitions depend upon our character and the values we have in life. We can have long—term goals and short—term goals. This is a lot like a football team. They may get four yards on the first play, and then three yards on the next play, with a short term goal of totaling ten yards for a first down. They then achieve this small goal over and over until they score a touchdown. And then they do it as many times as they can. Their long term goal is to win the ball game. Each time they execute a play, they seek to make the very best of that opportunity.

In the same way, our ambitions have an ultimate destination. What is yours? If, by achieving our goal, we make others happy and successful in Christ then that is even better. But if our ambitions hurt others, or drag someone down, we must revisit our plan and redefine our ambitions. It all depends on our level of contentment. What will make us feel happy? What will make us feel worthy, and what will make us feel powerful? It's all about what we want from life. If you want money, if money is your goal, you will compromise everything else to try to make more money. But if your ambition is to become an honest person and live a God-fearing life, no amount of money can attract you to do wrong or live in an ungodly manner. You can be the president of the largest chain of convenience stores in the state and still be honest and live for God. You can be a person that works for a house cleaning service and still be honest and live for God. No matter what your goals or ambitions, set them high and reach out for them so that you can be all that you can be for Christ. *Philippians 4:13* states *"I can do all things through Christ, who strengthens me."* Also note verse 19, *"But my God shall supply all your needs according to his riches in glory by Christ Jesus."* So if you have the strength, the promise, and the supplies from Almighty God backing you, set that goal and draw out your plan! With God by your side, the Word of God as your map, the Holy Spirit as your comfort, you cannot go wrong by trusting in Him.

Now let me ask you, is it biblical to have new goals? Is it biblical to have a set of new ambitions? Why should I have these new characteristics in my life? The answers to questions one and two are yes. If you do not set new goals and have new ambitions to reach those new goals, you will slide back into that same old life you were living before you came to Christ. A newborn Christian must understand his destination and how he travels in order to get there safely. *Psalm 1:1-6* clearly simplifies this travel. *"Blessed is the man who walketh not in the counsel of the ungodly, nor standeth in the way of sinners, nor sitteth in the seat of the scornful."* David clearly said that the man who stands around with or "hangs out" with sinners cannot and will not be blessed. You cannot rub against wet paint without getting it on you. You can be and live in the world without being of the world. God calls us to be and live differently and the only sure way to do this is to live by principles and principles alone. The "Blessed Ones" are people that live a principled, separated life. I know of many people that are lost, many people that drink, many people that may run off to ungodly places to have their fun but I have not sacrificed my principles or given in to the fleshly ungodliness because I know them. I live my life according to principles and stand on them until my life here is over. That is the one thing that makes me different and separated but it also is a testimony for God. I pray that my testimony will have an impact on those lost people I know and come in contact with each day. You too, must live by principles, not by personal preferences. A preference is what you choose and a principle is what you live.

Many young Christians get confused at the early stages of their Salvation. You may have recently accepted Christ into your heart and life. Please understand that, as a new Christian, you must tactfully and carefully seek God's direction in all we do and say. For an example, a fellow worker has come to you and, as you talk with each other, he offers you a cigarette. You can respond with, "I would not put a piece of that garbage to my mouth for anything" or you could just say, "No thanks, I don't smoke." The latter response will allow you to be accepted as more of a friend and as a witness than the first. You may work around lost and ungodly people but that does not take away your ability to live by principles. I have found that, in my life as a Christian in the work force, there are many times that people have a tendency to shy away from you because you may not drink, smoke, get involved with the dirty jokes or just feel they don't know what to say around you. That should be entirely acceptable and just know that your testimony shines and reflects a difference in your life when you are around them.

If you have asked Jesus to come into your heart and save you, then He did. Now, your new ambitions will prepare your life for new treasures and rewards ahead. A life of peace and serenity with God will also come with new goals and new ambitions.

"STARTING A FAMILY"

By R. Darryl Allgood

As a child, he seeks to remember, all the things he wished he had,
He cannot recall a home, to me that seems so sad.
He seeks to feel a history, a longing to be a part,
A union that is tied together, it is the longing within his heart.
Many years have passed him by now; he has grown into a man.
He wants to start a family, but does not how to begin.
The fear of all his childhood, the dark and dreary days,
It is almost like a ship at night, lingering in empty bays.
Just then, at the spur of a moment, a beam of light comes forth,
To direct the ship ashore, just turn and go due north.
This man has now a family, one he truly can adore,
He found the right foundation; it is God, the real and solid core.

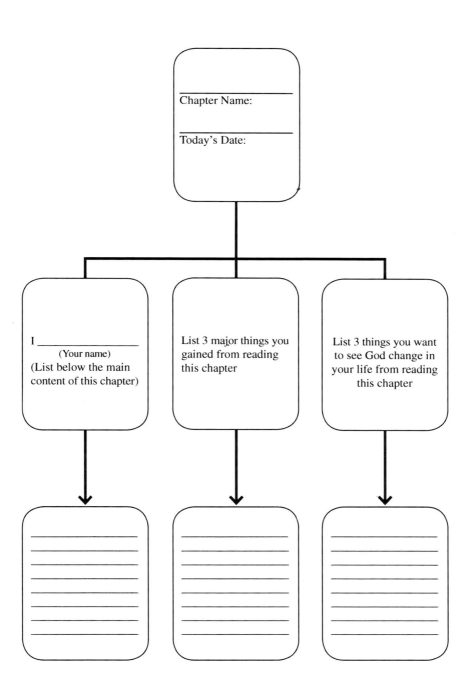

Chapter Name:

Today's Date:

I _____
(Your name)
(List below the main content of this chapter)

List 3 major things you gained from reading this chapter

List 3 things you want to see God change in your life from reading this chapter

CHAPTER 5

RETHINK YOUR THINKING

Read Psalms 51.1-10

Chapter 5

RETHINK YOUR THINKING

(Before continuing, stop and have a moment of prayer.)

David is teaching us about a penitent heart and is asking God to cleanse his innermost self from sin. David had much grief over his past and was pleading for God's mercy. In verse 10, David was asking God to create in him a clean heart. Three things must happen before anything can be created:

- *The Spirit of God must move upon the face of it. This is as He did in the beginning of time when God moved upon the face of the waters in Genesis 1:2. God made reference to the Holy Spirit and water many times because water is a symbol of washing and cleansing. The Spirit of God moved over the face of the waters and so must the Holy Spirit move within you.*
- *The word of God must speak to it. In the beginning, when there was nothing, God spoke every living thing into existence as well as the land and seas. His word is life and He is the Word. The creation of a clean heart can take place today but what about tomorrow? Our heart is human and made of flesh; therefore, when David said "renew a right spirit within me," he was saying that this is a daily routine and struggle. Each day, we must come boldly to the throne of grace and seek God's cleansing power and direction.*
- *The blood of Jesus Christ must wash it. The day we accepted Christ into our life, we asked Him to wash us and cleanse us from all unrighteousness. The important factor in God creating anything within us is that it is always perfect. When Jesus died on Calvary, He provided a perfect way of escape from sin. That is through His washing and cleansing and creating within us a clean spirit. The skill you and I must work on is the training or the "Rethinking of your thinking" process.*

Wipe out your old way of thinking. The first and foremost thing we must do in beginning this step is simple. We must stop thinking the way we used to think. The Bible tells us in *Proverbs 23:7 "as a man thinketh, so is he."* What you think, see and say is what you are. If you take a pitcher of fresh clean spring water with no contamination or added ingredients, and pour it into a clean larger container, you still have a clean batch of water. But the moment you add a little dirt here and a little dirt there, it has become polluted. After a period of time and more contamination, it becomes cloudy and unhealthy in appearance. Even if you purify the water by adding chemicals, it will never return to the pristine state it was in the beginning. Our mind and thoughts are the same. Every time a person views garbage, we can never remove it completely from our body and mind. It is permanently there.

This is why we must rethink our thinking. We can start by doing a complete inventory of our spiritual condition. In *verse 1 and 2*, David asked God to blot out his transgressions, wash him thoroughly from his iniquity, and cleanse all his sin. Remember that David was a man after God's own heart and, as he prayed, he knew God could see the most inner parts of his heart. That means David knew and felt God looking at his heart as though it was a glass house. The day you and I see our hearts and lives as a glass house is the day we see what God can see. As we kneel in prayer each day, our prayer should be as David prayed here in Chapter 51.

❖ *The Importance of the Word of God:*
Psalm 62:11

"God has spoken once, twice I have heard this: That power belongs to God." When we stop and realize how important the power of God is in our lives, and how it can transform us, we also have to realize where that power can be attained. It is stored in the Bible, the Word of God. If you and I want that perfect direction, that perfect peace and joy, we must go directly to the source of God's Word. In *Jeremiah 23:29, "Is not My word like a fire?"* says the LORD, *"And like a hammer that breaks the rock in pieces?"* I remember reading a while back that if we expect God to strengthen our spiritual lives; we have to go after it. We must pursue it as if it were gold. So when you ask me "How important is the Word of God?" I must respond to you, "Vitally."

One way to wipe out the old programs in a computer is to overwrite and replace them with new ones. It is similar for our New Life. All the years before now were lived outside of God so, keep in mind, it will take some time to get the old ways of thinking cleaned out. I admire the illustration that is used in drug and alcohol programs to help the ones that are addicted become sober and clean. Program participants are told that now, today; they must change their playground and change their play friends. In recovery programs, that is so very true. You cannot expect to stay sober or clean by continuing to run with the same crowd and do the same things; it will never work. I've been there and I personally know. You must change the way you think. Paul said in *Colossians 3:10, "And have put on the new man that is renewed in knowledge after the image of him that created him . . ."* God's word simply tells us that the way we start is by the replacing our old thoughts with the Word of God. We spoke earlier of reading the word of God each day and that is the first step. Our thoughts must also change and be cleaned up in order to get rid of the cloudiness and dirtiness. The importance of the Word of God is a must because it is the light in which our darkness is revealed.

Another area of assistance is scripture memorization. You may say, "I cannot memorize Bible verses." Trust me that you can if you put your mind to it. One of the best ways that I've found over the years is to write Bible verses on index cards and put them on my mirror in the bathroom. There, I can read and study them as I get dressed and ready every day. Or, place them on the refrigerator where we all go throughout the day or evening. I have put them on my toolbox. My wife gave me a Christian calendar that I placed on my desk. Other places that are visible at some point in the day will be equally effective. This is a tremendous help. The Bible said in *Proverbs 3:3, "Let not mercy and truth forsake you; Bind them around your neck, Write them on the tablet of your heart:"* This is a clear message that truth, being the Word of God, is the one successful tool to keep you secure in all you think, say, and do. Also, *Psalms 119:11, "Your word I have hidden in my heart that I might not sin against you."* There are many more verses in the Bible that reinforce the principle of God's Word being hidden, or memorized, within our life to keep us and strengthen our daily walk with God. Remember, we are rebuilding the foundation that you relied on for so long. As you read the Word of God daily, don't be alarmed by thinking you must remember every word you have read. As you read, the Holy Spirit is your guide and, as you live your daily life, the Holy Spirit will bring to mind just the right verse at the time you need it most. I never live a day without remembering some part of scripture I have read today, yesterday or even last month. As I read, I ask God to allow these passages to stick with me and guide me in all that I do.

❖ *The Importance of a Clear and Solid Decision*
Romans 6:13

"And do not present your members as instruments of unrighteousness to sin, but present yourselves to God as being alive from the dead, and your members as instruments of righteousness to God." You must decide today, in this very moment, which direction you are going to travel. In *Joshua 24:15*, it said *"Choose you this day whom you will serve . . ."* You must make a vividly clear decision and stand on that decision. The remaining part of that verse said, *". . . But as for me and my house, we will serve the Lord."* As Joshua was reviewing Israel's history, he called the tribes together and told them to make a choice. You and I cannot expect God to bless us by sitting on the fence, waiting to see which way the wind will blow, and then taking the way that is easy or pleasant. *Matthew 7:13-14* clearly tells us that many choose the wide and broad path, which is very easy to do, but which also leads to destruction. It takes a willing and open heart to listen to God and to allow the path God intends for us to follow to become our clear and solid decision. He said that, because the way is narrow and hard, only very few will go that way. Each day, God gives us enough grace and strength to make our journey, and He always will. *Philippians 4:19 "But my God shall supply ALL your need . . ."* If you make the decision to follow, He made the promise to supply.

Let me ask you several questions: Can you accept yourself without complaint? Can you love yourself at all times? And can you give and receive love? These questions are vitally important in your thinking process. These issues and personal goals can be worked on to develop a new way of thinking. I cannot help but remember a person in my younger years that thrived on other people's approval and on being accepted. This person would go to great lengths to do and say things, even though he may not have agreed with them, just to be approved by the gang or crowd. Let's look further at this area of our lives. There are many wasted minutes, days, months and even years trying to win someone's approval or overcome disapprovals we have encountered. We can begin by understanding that approval is a desire, not a necessity. We all enjoy compliments, praise and applause and it feels good to be stroked with these from time to time. But many people allow these to become a focus of their everyday life. This striving for approval is an area that must change within our lives. We will surely crash and burn if the approval of others remains our focus, but we will prosper and grow if we accept that we are what the perfect and mighty God made us to be. We must relax and accept we are what we are by the grace of God.

When we seek approval, the possibilities for truth then seem to vanish away. You have placed yourself in the position of not knowing what or who you are. You cannot state how you truly think or feel. You have to love yourself and accept yourself before you can begin to love someone else. God loved you and me before we were ever conceived because, as the old saying goes, God does not make junk. To escape this moose trap, we must understand the cultural war we live in. The fact is that our culture reinforces approval-seeking behavior as a standard way of life. When you make someone else's opinion and approval more important that your own, and when you don't get their approval, you have every reason to feel depressed, unworthy and guilty since you have made them more important than you. You and I have grown up in this society and, therefore, we have been tainted by this attribute. How do we overcome it? How do we defeat this pessimistic way of thinking? We have to change our way of thinking by replacing it with something else. Taking something away means replacing its void with something solid and everlasting. Remember the verse in *Proverbs 23:6-8, "Eat thou not the bread of him that hath an evil eye, neither desire thou his dainty meats: ⁷For as he thinketh in his heart, so is he: Eat and drink, saith he to thee; but his heart is not with thee. ⁸The morsel which thou hast eaten shalt thou vomit up, and lose thy sweet words."* The devil and all his minions are out there searching for one that will fall into his trap. God's promise is here in *Isaiah 31:4, "For thus hath the LORD spoken unto me, Like as the lion and the young lion roaring on his prey, when a multitude of shepherds is called forth against him, he will not be afraid of their voice, nor abase himself for the noise of them: so shall the LORD of hosts come down to fight for mount Zion, and for the hill thereof."* God has fought and won these battles already and, as you read these verses, think about what He has said. You must replace the old way of thinking with the Word of God. These solid and reliable principles build a true and solid foundation that, if storms or high waters come, will stand and stand strong successfully!

❖ *The Importance of a New Formula*
Luke 11:

The soul's hunger for wholeness may be inarticulate. We may be like small children crying in the middle of the night with no language but just a cry. This longing for rightness may be vocal but it is vague. When we leave ourselves at loose ends, we may get caught up in living loosely out of habit. Unless we conclude that the formulas used before do not work, we will continue to think, act and live the same exact way. Unless we think our way through to some definite conclusions; unless we follow a line of thought through and tie it with a knot of biblical convictions; our beliefs unravel into half truths and our temptations assail us. Straight, clean living requires some straight biblical thinking about God and His goodness. By keeping faith and the Word of God to guide us, we acquire the true formula needed to restructure our thought process.

Some of our most popular books on prayer treat it as if it were as easy as turning on the light switch. Just ask God for health, happiness, peace of mind and prosperity and, presto, it is done. As we will find out, it's not as simple as that. We must ask God, but we also must seek God in the places where He has revealed himself—the Holy Scriptures, the lives of saintly people, and in the quiet beauties of nature. This indeed takes time but, when prayer is treated as a time-saving device, it never becomes a life-saving force.

It has been said the following are the biggest enemies of our human nature: Fear, Regret, Greed, Ambition, Laziness, Self-Pity and Death. Among these, laziness is the most agreeable of all our enemies. Laziness can hang around the house all day and never get on our nerves. It is sometimes called by different names but, whatever we call it; it is the enemy that keeps our plans and ideas from working. However much we ask God, unless we seek Him with our whole mind, body, soul and strength, we will not find His answers to our prayers. God gives his highest to our utmost or greatest. Sometimes, it seems that God's door is closed to our requests. *Luke 11:* tells us the parable of the importunate man who had someone drop in on him unexpectedly after a long journey. Having no food for his guest, he went next door to his neighbor and knocked on his door at midnight seeking three loaves. The neighbor replied to him, saying not to trouble him at such an hour because it was late and his children were in bed with him. The Bible goes on to tell us that, because of the importunity of this man, the neighbor eventually did give him all he needed.

There is another thought to keep in mind; this parable is not designed to portray the nature of God, for God is never asleep or unaware nor does He ever get caught by surprise with all that is going on around us. The purpose of this parable is to teach us patience regarding what appear to be unanswered prayers and the need for persevering in our petitions. It can be that the door of a request remains closed until, like the importunate man, we use our hands and take action. That is why we say that the formula to which you are accustomed must be modified or altered to a more scriptural focus. The Bible promises us that those who thirst after righteousness "They shall be filled." Man is always hungering for way more than the world can give. The Bible says in *Luke 4:4, "Man shall not live by bread alone but by every word that proceeded out of the mouth of God."* Jesus taught that if we had enough to live on while depending on God before, then He would provide enough to live on today. That is what He meant when he said in *Luke 12:28-30, "If then God so clothes the grass, which today is in the field and tomorrow is thrown into the oven, how much more will He clothe you, O you of little faith? 29 "And do not seek what you should eat or what you should drink, nor have an anxious mind. 30 For all these things the nations of the world seek after, and your Father knows that you need these things."* This passage has always been a hard thing for practical men to accept. Look at the new bride and groom when all they need is each other and they are happy even though they may live in a very small apartment. When our minds are full of purpose, our lower hungers lose their urgency.

Have you ever had something so pressing to do that you had no desire to stop and eat and drink to keep your body going? That same type of desire is what we should have for the Word of God and for living a new life with a new foundation. That solid foundation is built of biblical principles that will never fail us. The principles described here will enable you to change your old way of thinking that has brought no long-lasting joy, happiness or peace of mind.

"THE NIGHT"

By R. Darryl Allgood

As the sun sets on the mountains and the skies turn out the grey,
The silence fills the midnight as the stars come out to stay.
You can start to hear the crickets, as a peace begins to flow,
Wild game begins to sleep as the moon puts off a glow.
Calmness covers the lakes as the breeze begins to rest,
God's creatures are more relaxed as they settle within their nests.
Small children are ready for bed as they have washed and brush their hair,
All snuggled and tucked inside, as they rest without a care.
The darkness is for a reason, it has a certain goal,
Without the proper rest, our body would take a toll.
The dark comes just in time, as God turns out the light,
We fall and drift asleep as we are always in His sight.
So when at night you wonder, why the darkness falls,
What is the final reason, why does it even call?
God always has a purpose; He always has a plan,
It was He that made the world, not the hand of mortal man.

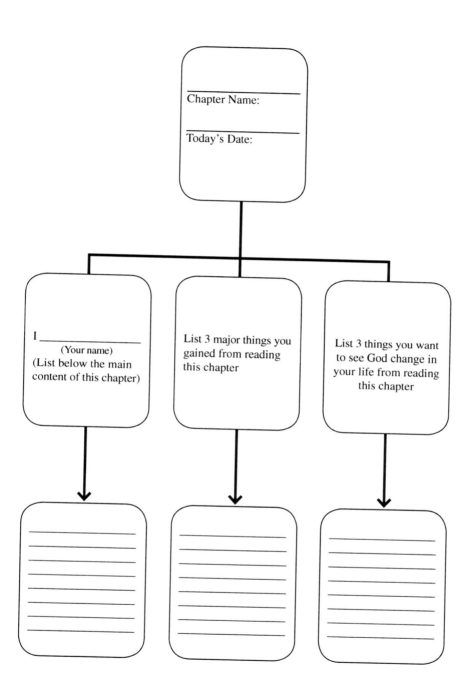

Chapter Name: _____

Today's Date: _____

I _____
(Your name)
(List below the main content of this chapter)

List 3 major things you gained from reading this chapter

List 3 things you want to see God change in your life from reading this chapter

CHAPTER 6

THE FORGIVENESS OF YOURSELF

Read John 8:32

Chapter 6

THE FORGIVENESS OF YOURSELF

(Before continuing, stop and have a moment of prayer.)

Have you ever been in a completely dark room and known if you could just make it to the light switch, all of your fear would be gone once you turned on the light? You walked and searched along each wall, trying to locate that one spot. After a while, it became draining, tiring, fearful and frustrating. This is the mark the unforgiving spirit leaves behind in our lives. The brightness of that one light can eliminate all of that unnecessary worry, pain and fear. But we don't allow it to. There is a tragic loss of lives each day simply because some are trapped in the inability to forgive themselves or others for past events or mistakes. They have convinced themselves their sin is way too great to be forgiven. Remember how you felt once the light was turned on in that pitch dark room? Before you found the switch, it seemed as if life had stopped. Then, within seconds, a light came on and a feeling of delight rushed through every vein in your body. The joy that comes from being forgiven is a pleasure like no other. To know that I have wronged someone is a miserable burden that never goes away until I have made it right and asked to be forgiven. There comes a great freedom in having forgiveness and no longer being in bondage to a life of unhappiness and misery. As you read the next several sections, pray as you review each one. Ask God to reveal each truth and principle to you and to help you accept and apply them to your daily life.

Psalms 103:10-12 is a tremendous assurance of God's forgiveness. *"He hath not dealt with us after our sins, nor rewarded us according to our iniquities. For as the heavens are high above the earth, so great is his mercy toward them that fear him. As far as the east is from the west, so far hath He removed our transgressions from us."* When God gave us complete forgiveness, he removed the sin to be remembered no more. That is the same as saying, "It never happened." So, if it never happened, what is there to feel guilty about? Our human conscience has a way of not allowing us to forget what we have done or said and we don't need to forget where we were brought from by the grace of God. You must accept His forgiveness so that you are not enslaved to a past that can never be changed. The past is the past and we only have the power to change the future by the Grace of God; with the power of God and his Holy Spirit.

❖ *Forgiving Yourself Successfully*
I John 1:9

This is the first step. If God; with all of his knowledge, abilities, love and mercy, can and has forgiven us of all of our transgressions, sin and actions, then use this same principle in realizing you don't need worry about forgiving yourself. God already has. You may say, "Why do the thoughts of all those things I used to do keep coming back to my mind? Does this mean I am not forgiven and that I need to ask God to forgive me again?" No, you do not. When God forgave you, he completely forgave you. *I John 1:9* said *"If we confess our sins, He is faithful and just to forgive us our sins, and cleanse us from all unrighteousness."* The word *cleanses* means to make clean. The dirt or sin is cleaned away; gone. The devil is the biggest deceiver and liar there has ever been and you must keep in mind that he wants nothing more than to convince you and me there are too many sins, too many mistakes, too dirty of a laundry basket. As long as you are hooked by this lie and deception, you will always be in his playground. The day you decided to give your heart and life to Christ was the day he lost grip on you. Remember, "Free and Free Indeed."

When a boy was about 12years old, out of the blue, his pastor called him up to the platform one night and ask him to sing "The Old Rugged Cross". He was an introverted teenager that was scared to death by this unexpected request. As he attempted to sing that song, his voice cracked and he quivered at the sight of all those people in the congregation. He began to cry and then went back to sit down on the front row of the church. He never forgot that day. Even though he is older now, he convinced himself that it is not possible to stand in front of a crowd much less attempt to sing a song in public for the rest of his life. He chose to be held in bondage for years and lost out on using a beautiful voice God bestowed upon him. In later years, he searched deep within his heart and soul and memorized *Philippians 4:13, "I can do all things through Christ which strengthens me."* Today, he has surrendered that bondage over to God and he stands and sings proudly and wonderfully because, in turning over the bondage to God, he has been released. There is no way we can ever undo where we have been, what we have done or what we have said. Those things, by the grace of God, have been and are forever forgiven and covered by the Blood of Jesus Christ. We must claim that promise daily. Paul said *Ephesians 6:10-12, "Finally, my brethren, be strong in the Lord and in the power of His might. ¹¹ Put on the whole armor of God that you may be able to stand against the wiles of the devil. ¹² For we do not wrestle against flesh and blood, but against principalities, against powers, against the rulers of the darkness of this age, against spiritual hosts of wickedness in the heavenly places."* What is that armor referring to? Paul, in many of his illustrations, used battle gear to refer to how we will spiritually conquer the world, the flesh and the devil. *Ephesians 6:12-20; "¹² For we do not wrestle against flesh and blood, but against principalities, against powers, against the rulers of the darkness of this age, against spiritual hosts of wickedness in the heavenly places. ¹³ Therefore take up the whole armor of God that you may be able to withstand in the evil day, and having done all, to stand. ¹⁴ Stand therefore, having girded your waist with truth, having put on the breastplate of righteousness, ¹⁵ and having shod your feet with the preparation of the gospel of peace; ¹⁶ above all, taking the shield of faith with which you will be able to quench all the fiery darts of the wicked one. ¹⁷ And take the helmet of salvation, and the sword of the Spirit, which is the word of God; ¹⁸ praying always with all prayer and supplication in the Spirit, being watchful to this end with all perseverance and supplication for all the saints ¹⁹ and for me, that utterance may be given to me, that I may open my mouth boldly to make known the mystery of the gospel, ²⁰ for which I am an ambassador in chains; that in it I may speak boldly, as I ought to speak.*

He first said we do not fight against something we can see. It is darkness where the devil hides and deceives us. If it were a physical thing such as a tree, we could take a chain saw and cut it into pieces and it is over. If it were a brick wall, we could take a stick of dynamite and blow it all apart. These are physical things that can be seen and then destroyed. Our problem would be over. But Paul says it is spiritual rulers of the darkness, so now the battleground and the weapons we must use are changed. He says we must take up the Whole Armor of God that we may be able to withstand the attack of the devil.

The Belt or Girdle was listed first. He said you must be *girded with truth*. That truth is the Word of God! The girdle was made of leather and was used to hold the sword and to gather up his tunic to keep from tripping in battle. It gathers all the other parts of his protective armor together. This is why you must first have the truth. A man or woman of integrity can face the enemy head on with no fear or doubts because we have the truth.

Secondly, he said the **Breastplate of Righteousness** is needed. The breastplate was made of metal and covered the soldier from the neck all the way down to the waist, front and back. This will fortify us as a child of God and, even from behind, we cannot be deceived by the devil. With our breastplate in place, we can withstand the devils attack. Without it, we are a moving target out in the wide open. When the devil accuses us, it is the righteousness of God that assures us of our salvation. Our position with Christ on a daily basis must be protected, and is protected as long as we daily understand the battleground we are on.

The Shodding of Feet: The Roman soldiers wore sandals that had the appearance of boots with nails sticking from the bottom to give them better footage, the ability to move more quickly, and support in long marches. As a child of God, we must make sure we take the guided path wherever we go. The most effective Christian is a witnessing Christian. I have always said that God can direct a moving arrow so much easier than one that is still in the quiver.

The Shield of Faith: A Roman shield was approximately four feet long by two feet wide. It was large enough to deflect fiery arrows, spears and rocks. The way the shield was designed, soldiers could connect one to the other, creating a marching wall and defending the entire line against assault from arrows. The faith in this passage refers to a living faith, an everyday practicing faith that knows the power of God in our lives is real and active.

The Helmet of Salvation is designed to protect our minds and our thoughts. The soldier had to protect his head from injury. His helmet was generally made of bronze and had cheek pieces to protect the face. Think back on how the devil defeated Eve. He made her believe that, just by eating of the forbidden fruit there was no harm. That brings us to where the bondage of not forgiving ourselves defeats us. God has provided you and me with all the essential tools and armor to defeat the lies and deceit of the devil. We can defeat the devil if we use these tools that God has given us.

Now, let's look back. Once we have a good and basic understanding of these principles, the Bible says in Acts 14:3, "Therefore they stayed there a long time, **speak**ing **boldly** in the Lord, who was bearing witness to the word of His grace, granting signs and wonders to be done by their hands." That means that we can say with confidence and boldness that we are forgiven and have been blessed by God!

In a parable, Jesus tells us that the pearl of great price was found by the man who was seeking goodly pearls. He sought for the truth; and in the course of his search, he found the one truth of all. In other words, the requirement for finding the truth is that you must be looking for it and want to find it. Deep down inside, you need to conquer this aspect of your life. *Romans 8:37-39* says *"Nay, in all these things we are more than conquerors through him that loved us."* As the man above was willing to search, you too must have a willing spirit to relinquish those past skeletons and allow them to be permanently buried. Keep in mind that the devil and this world desire you to be in bondage by these past actions. I personally use those things in my past to remind me of what God can do and what He has done in my own life. One of the hardest things to do is to forgive yourself. Remember, God's grace is greater than any and all of our sin.

Many people feel they have committed too great a sin or too many sins to be forgiven. They feel unforgivable. Sometimes, they feel the greater the sin, the less the forgiveness. That is a lie that the devil himself will try to entangle you with and, from that moment forward, bind you to misery. Others will cover it with the excuse of "I can never be anything great because of the degree of my sin." *Romans 6:14, "For sin shall not have dominion over you; for ye are not under the law but under grace."* Note also *verse 18, "Being, then, made free from sin, ye became the servants of righteousness."* When God provided the perfect forgiveness for us through the grace of His Son, he also provided a way to rise and live above the snare of failing to forgive yourself. The next time the devil brings up those past sins, change the channel through the Word of God. Tell him that sin does not have dominion over you and you refuse to accept his message or think thoughts. You must accept what God has done for you as fully completed. One way to do this is to write down a list of verses to use to reassure you of His promises. God's grace is always sufficient, no matter what has previously gone on in your life. The poem printed below describes God's perfect grace.

By not forgiving ourselves, we are creating a monster effect of disaster in every aspect of our life. We are implementing a self-made punishment that will steal, rob and imprison us and will infect other aspects of our life without even realizing it. Let me explain. When you refuse to forgive yourself, no matter what the sin may be, you are fertilizing a seed of discontentment. That seed will grow like a tumor with long tentacles stretching into every part of your life. Like a tumor, the tentacles may be attached to the kidney, the liver, the heart, the lung, or the pancreas. These are all major organs in the body that keep us functioning properly. Now, if we look at the other side of this illustration, the unforgiving spirit will affect our ability to enjoy love to the deepest and laughter to the fullest. We are walking around with this unmerited guilt that will surround us like a wall, restricting us from enjoying life at its fullest. You need to be as Joshua was and march right up to that wall and blow the horns and shout with the mighty shout, "God has forgiven me and I now forgive myself."

If you will first acknowledge God has forgiven you of all your sin and, second, accept His forgiveness for that sin, and third, believe with your whole heart that God remembers those sins no more, then you are free and free indeed. There is no debt for you to carry.

"SUFFICIENT GRACE"

By R. Darryl Allgood

Elijah in the Bible was a man of great strength,
Everywhere he did travel, he spoke with great length.
He always pointing upward, lifting up God's dear name,
Jesus is the Savior; the reliever of your pain.
Great deeds and wondrous actions, works and miracles too,
All because of God's grace, a life was made anew.
Sufficient grace each morning, sufficient grace each night,
Everywhere that you travel, we are always in His sight.
Never a darkened moment, we are left along the side,
Sufficient grace each moment, sufficient grace abides.
Now David was a small one, not that big if you recall,
He faced the huge Goliath, and the giant took the fall.
So when you feel bewildered, walked and spat upon,
Just be another David; just trust the Holy one.
He holds the every star, the moon, the sun and space,
The wonder of it all, His unchanging Sufficient Grace.
Sufficient grace each morning, sufficient grace each night,
Everywhere that you travel, we are always in His sight.
Never a darkened moment, we are left along the side,
Sufficient grace each moment, sufficient grace abides.

❖ *The Comfort of a Clean Conscience:*
John 15:11

When Jesus said in *Matthew 5:3, "Blessed are the poor in spirit, for theirs is the kingdom of heaven. ⁴Blessed are those who mourn, for they shall be comforted. ⁵Blessed are the meek, for they shall inherit the earth."* I feel He had sorrow for one's sin in mind. Perhaps that was his major emphasis, since he proclaimed blessing on "the poor in spirit." Yet, when we read these words about mourning, of what do we think first? Sorrow for our sins or sorrow for our losses and sufferings? I feel it is very much the latter. This fact reflects the current religious trend toward being more concerned with the evils that are set before us than with the sins we commit. Do you recall the times when there was a "mourner's bench" talked about? This was where church members would go in the earlier days and wait for divine pardon and forgiveness. Today, we more or less have a Psychology Clinic where one can come to unload their hearts with words. Let's look at where God said in *John 15:11 "These things I have spoken to you, that my joy may remain in you, and that your joy may be full.* His promise includes, in *John 15:3, "Now ye are clean through the word which I have spoken unto you."* Deep abiding comfort and joy come only to those with a clean and contrite or repentant heart. When I think of an illustration, I remember many years ago when I had done something wrong as a child and my parents had to punish me. It was not a pleasant feeling and, until I came to the point of telling my mother I was sorry and receiving her forgiveness, I was completely miserable. Once I did apologize, I had a peace and a serene feeling inside of me like a mighty rushing river flowing freely with no dam or rocks to stop it. I was forgiven and now I could go about my responsibilities and my life as I normally would. I did not think another minute about that incident. It was if it had never happened. Why is that? It was because first, I was wrong in what I had done. Second, I realized it took me going to my parents and apologizing and asking them to forgive me and third, I was completely forgiven. That settled it. I not only learned from it but I also did not have to carry a bad conscience around for hours, days, months and years. My parents never said another word about it to this day. I am fifty-two years old now and cannot even remember specific bad acts, but I do remember the forgiveness and the peace of mind it gave me.

There is another situation that did not end the same way. There was a man many years ago that carried the baggage of loneliness for a long time. At one point in his life this man was successful, very active in the community and holding ties with many people. But, at some point in his life, he went through an incident that caused hurt and pain and he became a hermit because of it. He became one that wanted not to be disturbed or bothered because of the possibility that he may be hurt again. So he built walls of defense which turned into loneliness and even bitterness. They became bondage and he carried this bondage with him every day of his life. Several years later, he finally came to a place where someone cared enough for his life; they shared the plan of salvation and the gift of God to him. He gave his life to Christ and, from that point forward, accepted God's love and complete forgiveness. He realized that he had lost many years to not having a clean and forgiving conscience. This is a trap that many people fall into. You may know someone who has fallen into this trap and are still held captive by it. By accepting the promises of God, we can escape this bondage and go forward with a clean and free conscience.

Lastly, let us leave this chapter with an illustration. It is only when displayed against dark velvet that diamonds show their true luster and beauty. It is in the darkness that we discover the richer values of life. Take my word, there is something more involved here than the oft-repeated truism that the night brings out the stars. The active principle is that when we face our sorrows and dig into our difficulties with spiritual guidance; we uncover the hidden riches of the secret places God has in store. *Psalm 91:1, "Whoever dwells in the shelter of the Most High will rest in the shadow of the Almighty.*

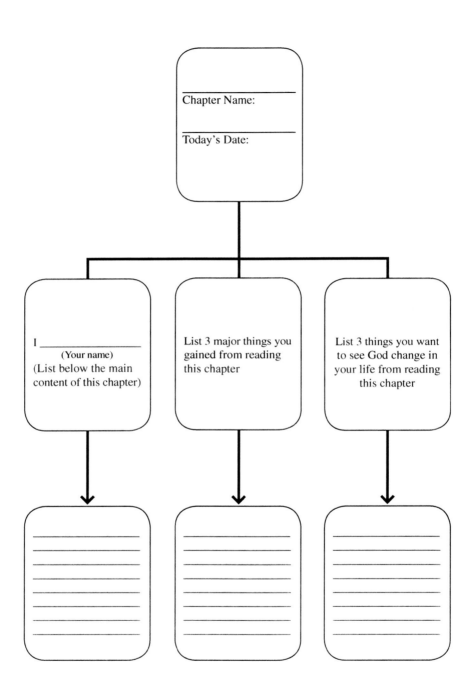

Chapter Name:

Today's Date:

I _____
(Your name)
(List below the main
content of this chapter)

List 3 major things you
gained from reading
this chapter

List 3 things you want
to see God change in
your life from reading
this chapter

CHAPTER 7

BE AWARE OF THE VALLEYS

Psalm 31:1-5

Chapter 7

BE AWARE OF THE VALLEYS

(Before continuing, stop and have a moment of prayer.)

Psalm 31:1-5, "In You, O LORD, I put my trust; Let me never be ashamed; Deliver me in your righteousness. Bow down Your ear to me, Deliver me speedily; Be my rock of refuge, a fortress of defense to save me. For you are my rock and my fortress; therefore, for your name's sake, lead me and guide me. ⁴ Pull me out of the net which they have secretly laid for me, for you are my strength. Into Your hand I commit my spirit; you have redeemed me, O LORD God of truth." As I read these verses, I can see the snares and the valleys that are lying out there just waiting for us to fall into them. The previous chapter described the way the devil lies even when everything seems so smooth and easy going. Remember the illustration of the darkness? We never see him coming and, because we know that tendency of the dirty little polecat, we must go a step further to place another layer onto your foundation.

Our human nature is to ride along under our own power as long as we think we have everything under control. We're human and that is our imperfect nature but once the lights go out or we find ourselves in such turbulence that it scares the wits out of us, we ask "What do I do now?" Don't be alarmed, for we have all been there at one point or another in our Christian life. Jonah was similar to us in that he wanted everything in his control and his own timing.

Let's study Jonah and his character. God told Jonah to go to Nineveh and preach to them that they might repent because they were so wicked. God told Jonah if the Ninevites did not repent, He would surely destroy the city. Although Jonah did not want to go, he went anyway, hating every moment of the travel. Let's not forget, according to Jonah, he was on the right path headed to exactly the place God told him to go. So in Jonah's eyes, he was doing and following God's perfect lead.

Once he arrived and preached the gospel and the Ninevites repented, Jonah became enraged. He was totally upset that God did not keep His end of the bargain in Jonah's eyes. Jonah was one that wanted control at his time in his way. How many of us fall into that way of thinking?

Let's look at why Jonah fell into the devil's trap and landed in a spiritual valley:

- His Spirit was wrong all the way to Nineveh.
- He pictured in his mind God destroying Nineveh, even if they did repent.
- He hated the little boat he had to travel on to get there.
- He was in a raging storm and almost drowned in the waves.
- He spent three turbulent days in the nasty belly of a great fish.

These things are not what you want to write home about or take pictures of and show on a slide or even brag to your friends about. So, when the Ninevites did repent, that did not make him happy. I am sure he imagined pushing the button himself to allow the fire and brimstone fall down onto the city. That was not God's plan. Rather the salvaging of those people's lives was what God wanted. Jonah became so mad, he went outside the city and sat down on the side of the road and the Bible tells us a plant grew tall enough to give him shade. He was still angry as he sat in the shade and the sun baked down. He sat there waiting to see what would happen to the city next. He was disillusioned, and then the plant died and removed the shade from him. And Jonah was more concerned about the death of his shade plant than he was about the potential death of all the Ninevites. Jonah's inability to recognize God's sovereignty lead to Jonah placing himself above God. Jonah felt he knew best but, what he actually did was fall into the trap the devil prepared for him and it caused a separation in the relationship of God and Jonah.

The valleys in life will always come. We never know when or even why. By being prepared to place these principles in our lives and to rely on them, we disarm old slew foot and use the weapons of defense in our lives. There are many days that are great, super and magnificent, but there are also those times when it seems every day is a Monday. Nothing seems to go right for us, just as nothing went right in Jonah's life. Let me remind you of *Romans 8:37-39, "Yet in all these things we are more than conquerors through Him who loved us. 38 For I am persuaded that neither death nor life, nor angels nor principalities nor powers, nor things present nor things to come, 39 nor height nor depth, nor any other created thing, shall be able to separate us from the love of God which is in Christ Jesus our Lord.* Being in the valley is the time we must realize we are weak and unable to stand alone and we must know God's promise to always be true and strong enough for any test that comes our way.

❖ *In the Valley, God is our Refuge:*
Psalms 46:1-2

"God is our refuge and strength, a very present help in trouble. ² Therefore we will not fear, Even though the earth be removed, And though the mountains be carried into the midst of the sea;" We must understand that there are days when it seems the valley is long, dark and lonely. You may think the troubles and heartaches are just way too heavy to bear. There are times when God looks down and can see a valley is needed in our life. Why? What is the reason? Think of the passage *Psalm 57:1, "Be merciful to me, O God, be merciful to me! For my soul trusts in You; And in the shadow of your wings I will make my refuge, until these calamities have passed by."* David had fled into a cave to escape from Saul who was out to destroy him. You and I are as human as David. He was fearful but he knew where to draw his strength and he knew God was his protector. It was here that David saw that God was his refuge even though he was scared. The human aspects of our lives are no different from those of others. But, when you and I enter into a valley, we don't have to be alarmed because we know and trust that God knows exactly what He is doing. It is in our weakest moments that God's strength is made strong in our lives. It will take valleys in our life to reassure us of this promise. *II Corinthians 12: 9-10, "And He said to me, "My grace is sufficient for you, for My strength is made perfect in weakness. Therefore most gladly I will rather boast in my infirmities, that the power of Christ may rest upon me. ¹⁰ Therefore I take pleasure in infirmities, in reproaches, in needs, in persecutions, in distresses, for Christ's sake. For when I am weak, then I am strong."* When you find yourself in the valley, just remember the old gospel song wrote by Connie Smith, *"In the valley, He restores my soul."* There are some mountains we were not made to climb and, because of that, we are not self-sufficient but must be dependent on God and God alone. God's design is never to harm, hurt or destroy but to lift us up and place our feet on solid foundations. God saw that a flood was

needed and, because of God's perfect love and plan, He advised Noah to build the ark. How do you think Noah must have felt when he set out to follow God's instruction and build an ark in a desert? Do you think you and I would have responded as he did? Not only are we to know God's will but we are act on it as well. The promise of God is to be our refuge and so God gave to Noah the one thing that would be a symbol of His refuge, the ark.

❖ Our Valleys Are Some of God's Greatest Works:
1 Kings 20:27-29

"And the children of Israel were mustered and given provisions, and they went against them. Now the children of Israel encamped before them like two little flocks of goats, while the Syrians filled the countryside. [28] *Then a man of God came and spoke to the king of Israel, and said, "Thus says the LORD: 'Because the Syrians have said, "The LORD is God of the hills, but He is not God of the valleys," therefore I will deliver all this great multitude into your hand, and you shall know that I am the LORD.'"* [29] *And they encamped opposite each other for seven days. So it was that on the seventh day the battle was joined; and the children of Israel killed one hundred thousand foot soldiers of the Syrians in one day."* The valley was the victory for the children of Israel but they did not even know it. God sent an angel to the King of Israel and informed him that the Syrians were so confident that God was only the God of the mountains and not the valleys that they were sending soldiers into battle. Led by God, the children of Israel set up their camp on the opposite side of the valley in preparation for them. When the time was right, they killed 100,000 soldiers in one day. The rest ran to the city of Aphek where a wall fell on the 27,000 remaining warriors. The valley in the verses became the scene of one of the greatest victories in their lives.

Don't ever be alarmed for when you know you are where God wants you, His principles will never fail and He is never late! There is a victory promised by God that will soon arrive. When it does, you will be assured once again that God does know what He is doing each and every second of the day.

Paul in the New Testament was in prison many times and, to him, this was a great valley. As you stop and think; the best words he put to paper was at these times. Paul could not see what this purpose was but God did. Paul was a man of vision but he also was a man of action. Paul devoted himself single-mindedly to fulfilling the commission entrusted to him on the Damascus road and laboring more abundantly than all of his fellow apostles. Paul was a great letter writer and you can see his personality in his writings. As you read and study the Bible, you will see that Paul created great literature while imprisoned.

We cannot wrap up our life into neat little physical, emotional, intellectual and spiritual packages. We do physical things at certain times and then also have times for emotional activities. We cannot forget the intellectual moments and then have our spiritual times. All of these make up the wholeness or the brokenness of us. Look at the circle below and notice the small blocks representing our physical, emotional, intellectual and spiritual make up. Do you see the smaller circle with a cross in the middle? This represents Christ living within our heart and life. The larger of the two represents our human nature and follows the natural leadings of the four aspects of our life. Whichever of the two circles is larger determines how we handle situations and circumstances in our lives. It's as if you have both arms extended: one arm extended to the right has a grip on a rope that is being pulled to the right and the other arm is extended to the left and has a grip on a rope that is being pulled to the left. Whichever arm is the weakest is the one that will give first. Our spiritual growth is vitally important in the valleys as well as throughout our daily Christian lives. As we place these principles in and make them a part of our everyday lives, you will see the smaller of the circles become larger and the trials that come into our lives will not seem so big after all.

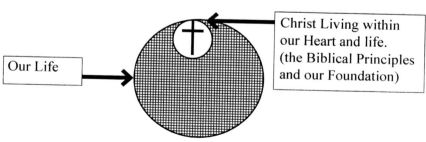

Our Life

Christ Living within our Heart and life. (the Biblical Principles and our Foundation)

As I was driving through town several days ago, I noticed a person running along the road. He seemed so tired yet was still running as if the end of his race was just around the corner. As I thought of this runner, I pictured the days upon days he would train. Arising early in the morning, when others were still resting, he would stretch his muscles and prepare for the distance he would be running. As he runs, he points toward the goal he will reach before he calls his run complete. Along the way, he struggles with breathing but focuses on taking one breath at a time, then another and another until he reaches the finishing point of his run. At the end of the exercise, no matter how tired he may be, he has accomplished the distance set out to run. At last," he cries, "the race for today is complete." In our lives, we too, face a race or a struggle each day, whether our job, family, medical situation or just spiritual warfare. Our method should also be breathing one breath at a time or one day at a time. In our hearts, we may think we cannot make it another step but, in reality, as we start to take one breath as it comes, we find ourselves making it further down the road of life than we thought possible. God said in *Psalm 91:1 "He that dwelleth in the secret place of the Most High shall abide under the shadow of the Almighty."* Walking in one's shadow means to be very, very close to that person. God's promise is just that type of walk. The place He is referring to is our daily prayers and our ongoing trust in His perfect plan and strength. This is no secret, but so few can comprehend his real love and peace. Why? The reason is not that we don't want to understand, but rather is because our lives have so many new trials that we must willingly choose to trust Him each new day. You and I are made of the flesh and so we make mistakes each day. Like the runner, sometimes we forget to breathe or maybe we just breathe incorrectly. God has promised never to leave his children nor forsake them. He is always there, no matter what worry may come. Always keep in mind, taking that one breath at a time and, before you know it, the race is complete for the day. The worry and fear of defeat that was so pressing upon our heart and mind has been conquered and the race was run with perfect strength and grace. We were able to stand again, just as God promised. One breath at a time as each new mile we face, enabling us to reach our finish line each day.

"THE FAWN IN THE FOLD"

By R. Darryl Allgood

As the morning was breaking and the air was so fresh,
The body awakened from a long needed rest.
The deer and the fawn so innocent and free,
Now moving and grazing, for their appetites appease.
All of a sudden from very deep within,
Came howling, a wailing, like a screeching violin.
The dogs were now trailing, their scent now so fresh:
For the quest of a challenge like a huge college test.
The deer and fawn quickly jumped to beware;
The deer gave her life for her young she did bear.
Now the fawn continues to journey, its life to protect;
But the dogs keep coming for its life bound to wreck.
It leaps; it runs and dodges for a while,
It seems like forever and millions of miles.
God's love so tender, so rich, and so deep;
It is able to sustain, to protect, and to keep.
As the fawn has now traveled, so long and so hard,
He crosses the valley with his wounds and his scars.
The dogs, now so close and hot on its trail;
The fawn is so weary and ready to fail.
Then out from the heaven, where God stands and can see
He reaches the fawn and issues a decree.
"It is I the Lord God, the creator of all.
The earth and the moon and the huge waterfalls."
Now His arms are so strong, so loving, and true,
The decree was His son, for me and for you.
The dogs with their goal, to destroy and to dismay
Must now turn and run, for their master to obey.
Never be alarmed when times dark and so cold,
Just trust in the master as the fawn in the fold.

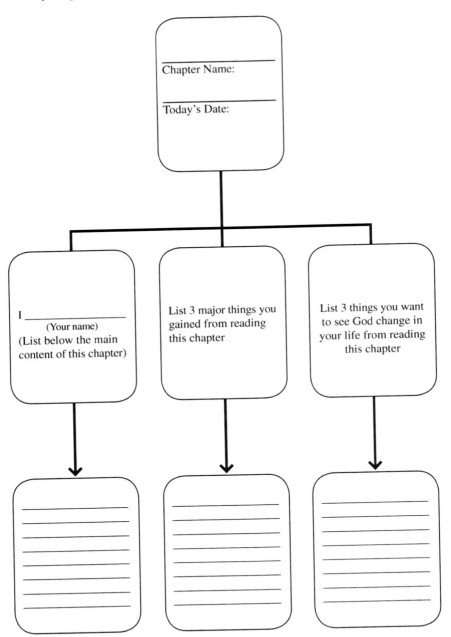

Chapter Name:

Today's Date:

I _____
(Your name)
(List below the main content of this chapter)

List 3 major things you gained from reading this chapter

List 3 things you want to see God change in your life from reading this chapter

CLAIMING YOUR MOUNTAIN

Isaiah 40:31

Chapter 8

CLAIMING YOUR MOUNTAIN

(Before continuing, stop and have a moment of prayer.)

There was a story I heard years ago of a man that was walking through the mountains when he discovered an eagles' nest among the rocks of a high ledge. The mother was not there so he reached inside the nest, picked up one of the eggs, and took it with him. When he arrived home, he went to his chicken house where there were mother hens sitting on their eggs, waiting for them to hatch. The man reached down and placed the eagle egg under one of the mother hens. After some time passed, the eggs all hatched, including the eaglet. The chicks and the eaglet were fed by the mother hen, and there seemed to be no difference among them. As they continued to grow, the eaglet outgrew the little chicks by a huge amount. One day, as they were walking around the pen, the eaglet lifted her beak towards the heavens, spread her wings and took off toward the heavens.

Like the eagle, we as human beings created by God have been endowed with certain inherent possibilities. Through God's enabling power, we can rise above the marsh vapor of problems that comes our way and scale new heights and achieve victories like never before. God's promise is never failing and I treasure so much this verse in *Isaiah 40:31*, *"But they that wait upon the Lord shall mount up with wings as eagles; they shall run and not be weary, and they shall walk and not faint . . ."*

James tells us *1:2-4, "My brethren, count it all joy when you fall into various trials knowing that the testing of your faith produces patience. ⁴ But let patience have its perfect work, that you may be perfect and complete, lacking nothing."* Any one of us can handle fifteen to twenty minutes of a struggle, or maybe even a day or two, but what about a week or even months? James is talking about a long term period that will instill within us a faith and trust in God that will last us a lifetime. Being on that journey through the valleys is hard and stressful, and sometimes brings heartaches, but God teaches us through these times that the claiming of your mountain will be that much more of a triumph. I am reminded of something I read that said; "Perfect Trust brings Perfect Results."

When you are not on the mountain top, you are usually going through an intermediate stage that will last for while but then send us back into a different valley. James told us in 1:12: *"Blessed is the man who endures temptation; for when he has been approved, he will receive the crown of life which the Lord has promised to those who love Him."* James was telling us that, when we persevere through these valleys and problems that have come into our lives, God will in return give to us a certain insight and wisdom that others wonder about and desire to have. The valleys are required in order to claim our mountain. I remember as a child singing a song that goes like this: "I want that Mountain, I want that Mountain, where the grapes of cluster grow, where the milk and honey flow. I want that mountain, I want that mountain. I want that mountain that my Lord has promised me."

❖ *Be Content With Where You Are:*
Hebrews 13:5

Don't be alarmed by or confused with this sectional title. There is a big, big difference between being content and being satisfied. As you stop and consider your position in life and your surroundings, be aware of where you are exactly. A good illustration of this would be the trip we planned to Hawaii earlier in the book. Our journey has been laid out and we know we are leaving from here and making a trip to there. We do not know what the roads are going to be like, whether they will be smooth or rough. We don't know what the weather will bring, sunshine or rain. Our transportation may encounter a flat tire or an oil leak or maybe no problems at all. It will entail bridges, highways, gas stations, eating, sleeping and even the airport. You are content when stopping for gas but not yet satisfied. You are content on the highways but not yet satisfied. You are not *completely satisfied* until you actually arrive in Hawaii and your feet touch the ground that you have tarried, worked, sweated, slept and awaited for so long. That plan and work and wait is satisfied and so you rejoice once you arrive. That is what we are talking about here; just be content and don't stop until you step on top of that mountain. There will be rainy days and there will be big storms.

Don't worry or fret because you already know who your pilot is and He has promised never to leave or forsake you, *Hebrews 13:5; "Let your conduct be without covetousness; be content with such things as you have. For He Himself has said, "I will never leave you nor forsake you."* Patience is a very hard subject to talk about but it is part of our daily lives, no matter who we are. The contentment we must have is not easy with the generation we live in when all is instant gratification. The microwaves and internet gives us exactly what we want when we want it. The Bible clearly teaches us waiting or patience is a virtue (a desirable quality). I think we can all agree that patience is one of the hardest parts of our Christian living. *Psalms 27:14, "Wait on the LORD; Be of good courage, And He shall strengthen your heart; Wait, I say, on the LORD! Psalms 37:9, "For evildoers shall be cut off; But those who wait on the LORD, They shall inherit the earth."* These passages give us comfort and the assurance that waiting on God for His perfect timing gives the promise that we shall reap the victory of the mountain top.

What if choosing to be content is based on how you feel? Today, I feel happy and joyful so I will be content, right? Tomorrow I wake up and the world has turned upside down and all that can go wrong has gone that way. Are you still content? Feelings are not just emotions but are reactions we choose to have. Self-defeating reactions can come from not having a clear plan. Each day can be new and brings contentment with it because you have predetermined that God is in control of your life and the devil is not going to bring defeat. There is a freedom that comes with knowing God is working within me and God is also growing me. This is progress and these are the steps to claiming your mountain each and every time.

❖ *Allow God's Growth Within You:*
II Corinthians 4:16

As young children grow up, they go through stages where their clothes and their shoes get too small. It may get to the point the clothes become tight and buttons may break off or pants will tear. In any case, it is time to go shopping for new ones. Let's look at our Christian life in this same manner. Our Christian growth is in some ways just like this growth of the child. *II Corinthians 4:16, "Therefore we do not lose heart. Even though our outward man is perishing, yet the inward man is being renewed day by day."* As a child grows, he becomes larger; little by little. When living by Christian principles, we inwardly grow little by little to a point where God desires to give us new things and the new blessings that He has promised.

Claiming the mountain in your life requires the acknowledgement of growth. Each test and trial you go through matures you more and more. Another assurance was given to us by the Apostle Paul in *Philippians 3:13-14, "Brethren, I do not count myself to have apprehended; but one thing I do, forgetting those things which are behind and reaching forward to those things which are ahead,* [14] *I press toward the goal for the prize of the upward call of God in Christ Jesus."* The gratification that comes from knowing you are growing drives out the gloominess and gives you a sweet peace that God has all in His control. Remember this, as long as you are growing, you are not failing and growth implies you are improving. Stronger and stronger is always God plan for us. The two great laws of life are growth and death. If we are not growing, that is another way to say we are dying. Which do you choose? I want to grow and be headed for a master goal. Through the application of these principles in our daily lives, we can and will get there. Growth in the Christian life gives melody and a peace that passes all understanding.

I once heard a story of an excellent and accomplished marksman traveling through a community where he saw evidence of some amazing shooting. On barns, trees and fence posts he saw targets posted with a bullet hole dead center in the target. Time after time, it was a perfect bull's eye hit. He was amazed by this shooting; he went on a search to find the marksman that had this talent. He finally met the man and his first statement was "You are the best I have ever met. What do you give the credit to for being so good?" The man then responded, "I shot first and then drew my target." Many people fail to reach that mountain top simply for not aiming. We live in a generation that believes in short cuts to everything in life. What is the quickest way so I can bypass the growing stage and I can just arrive? In order to make the most out of our lives, we must first aim at where we want to go.

The Apostle Paul gave witness to the difference between the goal and the achievement in the reference above. If we fail to grow we live with regret later in life and lose out on some of the greatest rewards God wants to give us. We find ourselves saying "If I'd only . . . ." so many times. Don't be one of those that find themselves failing to grow due to fear of not knowing the final outcome. With no goal or no aim, where are you headed and where will you end up? The greatest truths, and I mean eternal truths, cannot be learned by mere investigations and study. They are not truths that come from reasoning and seeing if they match what the encyclopedia says. These truths come from life being lived and the world being seen in a surrendered trust with God each day of our life.

"It Only Takes a Moment"

By R. Darryl Allgood

When it seems that you have traveled your last weary mile,
Your body is oh so tired and you want to rest awhile.
You glance for just one look to see if you are alone,
Then dial on heavens phone, you no longer want to roam.
You quickly get an answer; the voice is loud and clear,
There is no way question; you lose all sense of fear.
You can hear the angels singing, a peace of love divine,
The bells are loudly ringing the perfect timely chime.
He speaks with love so tender; a voice of care so true,
It has to me my father, he said "Child is that you?"
You finally dialed that number; you no longer want to wait,
You took the right road now, you see the golden gates.
It only takes a moment to make a phone call home,
It only takes a moment, are you tired of being alone?
He's always glad to hear, to talk or just be there,
It only takes a moment, your burden He wants to bear.
Don't ever be alarmed, frightened or just dismayed,
It only takes a moment; he turns your night to day.

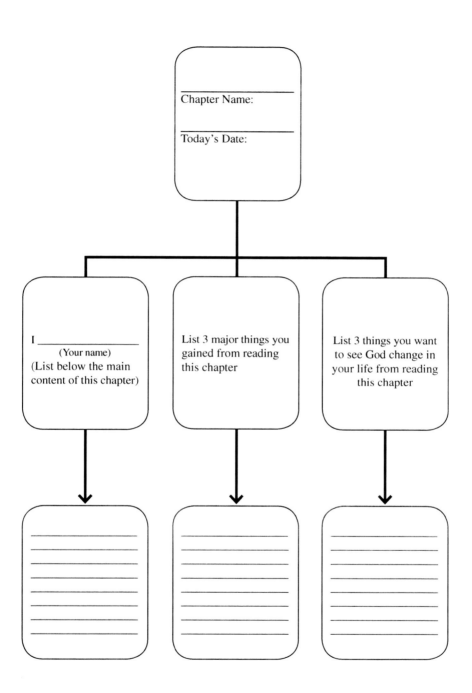

Chapter Name:

Today's Date:

I _____
(Your name)
(List below the main content of this chapter)

List 3 major things you gained from reading this chapter

List 3 things you want to see God change in your life from reading this chapter

CONCLUSION

A Biblical Start To Solid Foundations

In closing, let's remember where you started and where you are today. The life we choose and the decisions we make will alter our results in the Christian walk. The reason Christ came to this earth was because we are human and imperfect. Therefore, we make mistakes; we have regrets and will always be targeted by the great deceiver, the devil. As long as we know this, we have the upper hand simply because of the cross at Calvary and the power of God. The Bible said in *1 John 4:4, "You are of God, little children, and have overcome them, because He who is in you is greater than he who is in the world."* The promise of God is always greater than pleasures of a season. For, you see, the pleasures of the season will come to an end when compared to an eternity that has no end.

Back in Chapter One we learned we have to experience true salvation through Jesus Christ our Lord. Once we have done this, our next step is making a public profession declaring our faith. *Matthew 10:32-33, "Therefore whoever confesses me before men, him I will also confess before My Father who is in heaven" But whoever denies me before men, him I will also deny before My Father who is in heaven."* Baptism is an act of obedience that declares one's faith. *Acts 2:37-38, "Now when they heard this, they were cut to the heart, and said to Peter and the rest of the apostles, "Men and brethren, what shall we do?"*

38 Then Peter said to them, "Repent, and let every one of you be baptized in the name of Jesus Christ for the remission of sins; and you shall receive the gift of the Holy Spirit." You'll want to study the Bible and share Jesus with others as well. Learn to pray, be faithful to church and trust Christ to direct you in every aspect of your life.

When you have the New Birth and have started New Walks; you're Building New Truths for you have a New Life. As you see, the one is built on the other and eventually your life develops into a testimony of God's working power and promise. Each and every truth in God's Word is a treasure waiting to be discovered by you and me. One of the principles revealed in God's Word is that we are created to grow and develop as in Gen. 1:28. He told Adam to go out, grow and multiply. Our life contains critical times and incidents and even relationships that makes us who we are. That does not mean we are doomed to defeat or failure. We have the ability to choose don't we?

Another principle we learn from Gods Word is that we need relationships. Let's look at how and why God created us. God created Adam and Eve for what reason? To praise Him and to have companionship is the answer to that question. The joy and completeness we have with our spouse cannot and will never be replaced with anything else, no matter where you search. When one spouse is away from the other spouse for a certain amount of time, they begin to feel incomplete and cannot wait until they see each other again. That is the same way God is with us. He wants on our relationship and fellowship with Him to be fresh daily. He wants us to come to Him each day for strength, true joy and a renewed zeal.

When we stop and look at true forgiveness, I cannot help but think of the Prodigal son and how he wasted every penny that his father had given him. It was gone! But yet, after a while when the son realized his mistake; he went back home. When the father saw his son afar off, he did not think of wasted money or foolishness of the son but only of his love and the restored relationship between the son and the father. When God forgave you and me, he did it completely and not half way. Forgiving yourself and others will release the hold the devil has on you completely. Don't be imprisoned by things of the devil in your life; rather, turn it over to God and be free, yes free indeed. Today, right this very moment, commit that from this point forward you will be a Christian and child of God with a Biblical and Solid Foundation that does not crumble in this world of shaky grounds.

The next section has fifteen of the most heart-touching and uplifting poems written by the author. Some were placed in the earlier part of "A Biblical Start to Solid Foundations" and others are found only here. May God bless you on your new journey and may the following section of poems be a tremendous blessing and encouragement.

RHYMES FOR TIMES
BY R. DARRYL ALLGOOD

"GIVE YOUR HEART"

Written by R. Darryl Allgood

No time for family values, no time to stop and pray
No time to say "I love you" is now the American way.
Children are fighting their family members and death at every hand
Divorce is not the answer even though they say you can.
It seems your heart is broken, it hurts and aches inside
He tells you "Turn it over", this is what you'll truly find.
Just give your heart to Jesus, there is trust with me today
Just give your heart to Jesus, I will never, ever stray.
I have traveled the road you're on, I've been that way before
Just give your heart to Jesus, the end of pain and war.
Now battles will come and go, and valleys great and small
it will seem you're out of strength, the verge to tilt and fall.
When you feel that no one loves you and all have run away
He'll wrap His arms around you and say I'm here to stay.
God keeps you safe at night though dark and soar afraid
you will sleep through all the storms to find another day.

"The Night"

Written by R. Darryl Allgood

As the sun sets on the mountains and the skies turn out the grey,
The silence fills the midnight as the stars come out to stay.
You can start to hear the crickets, as a peace begins to flow,
Wild game begins to sleep as the moon puts off a glow.
Calmness covers the lakes as the breeze begins to rest,
God's creatures are more relaxed as they settle within their nests.
Small children are ready for bed as they have washed and brush their hair,
All snuggled and tucked inside, as they rest without a care.
The darkness is for a reason, it has a certain goal,
Without the proper rest, our body would take a toll.
The dark comes just in time, as God turns out the light,
We fall and drift asleep as we are always in His sight.
So when at night you wonder, why the darkness falls,
What is the final reason, why does it even call?
God always has a purpose; He always has a plan,
It was He that made the world, not the hand of mortal man.

"The Fawn in the Fold"
Written by R. Darryl Allgood

As the morning was breaking and the air was so fresh,
The body awakened from a long needed rest.
The deer and the fawn so innocent and free,
Now moving and grazing, for their appetites appease.
All of a sudden from very deep within,
Came howling, a wailing, like a screeching violin.
The dogs were now trailing, their scent now so fresh:
For the quest of a challenge like a huge college test.
The deer and fawn quickly jumped to beware;
The deer gave her life for her young she did bear.
Now the fawn continues to journey, its life to protect;
But the dogs keep coming for its life bound to wreck.
It leaps; it runs and dodges for a while,
It seems like forever and millions of miles.
God's love so tender, so rich, and so deep;
It is able to sustain, to protect, and to keep.
As the fawn has now traveled, so long and so hard,
He crosses the valley with his wounds and his scars.
The dogs, now so close and hot on its trail;
The fawn is so weary and ready to fail.
Then out from the heaven, where God stands and can see
He reaches the fawn and issues a decree.
"It is I the Lord God, the creator of all.
The earth and the moon and the huge waterfalls."
Now His arms are so strong, so loving, and true,
The decree was His son, for me and for you.
The dogs with their goal, to destroy and to dismay
Must now turn and run, for their master to obey.
Never be alarmed when times dark and so cold,
Just trust in the master as the fawn in the fold.

"BECAUSE OF LEE"

Written by R. Darryl Allgood

I have run so long, with my guilt and my shame,
The hurt in my heart, I cannot explain.
No dream or purpose have ever I known,
My life, my family, and all that I own.
All wasted and gone, dwindled away,
Not knowing the answer is all I can say.
A knock at my door one dark gloomy morn,
A child appeared, clothes withered and worn.
With a smile of contentment, happy with glee,
He gave me a tract and said "My name is Lee."
"Thank you," I said, as he went on his way,
He shouted, "He took it" on this one Christmas day.
I pondered a moment and thought for a while,
"Maybe this is it" as I spoke out loud.
I decided to read it, what have I to lose,
It's better to read, rather sit here and snooze.
A plan so warm, so loving, and kind,
I could not believe it was here all the time.
Transforming and wonderful it was all to me,
Simply because of a boy named Lee.
Years have passed since that wonderful day,
That little boy Lee has now passed away.
He yielded his life and obeyed a call,
Not knowing my life had reached a wall.
It is I now knocking from door to door,
Giving the plan to all rich and the poor.
I am very grateful for the willingness you see,
For I would not be here had it not been for Lee.

"BABIES DON'T QUIT"

Written by R. Darryl Allgood

A small child, growing up in stages, has never known fear or being afraid as he attempts new things each day of his life. I can remember when my first child was taken to his grandparents at his crawling and slowly walking stage. He would hold to the coffee table and work his way around it, touching and even trying to pick up things he had never seen before. When he turned loose of the table and attempted to walk away, he would fall and roll over, but would get back on his knees and work his way back to the coffee table and try it again and again. He finally was able to walk away from the table with more stability and strength than he had before.

Now, he is in his early twenties and a senior in college. Years have passed since he was that small and I know, as a parent, we all can agree to similar stories as this. There is another area of these stories we tend to overlook. Our lives as young or older adults can be halted due to a trial or tragedy that has arrived in our path. We attempt to face it with strength, but with our strength and not God's. We approach the table as the small child does and when we turn loose, we do well for a second or two, but we then tumble and fall down and begin to worry, fret and then realize, "Hey, let's try it again." This time, we attempt it with more caution and a better understanding of what is needed to make it work with more and added strength. This comes with time and practice, not forgetting patience and endurance. I like the old saying by Timex Watches, "They take a licking and keep on ticking." That philosophy can be adopted by each of us as well. The life we live will always have obstacles, bumps and even potholes, but that is ok and acceptable as long as we remember this one thought—even though we fall, face a major crisis or some other event, we can get up, make up our mind as that child did and go full speed ahead. It's ok that we fall or stumble along the way; this is our learning process which, in return, will bring us wisdom. Therefore, we too are the babies that don't quit.

"PERFECT STRENGTH"

Written by R. Darryl Allgood

People say that they can make it; they rely upon their strength,
No need for Bible direction, they're strong though never weak.
But then a sudden crash, as life drops to the ground,
Thinking all is lost and over, pondering on heaven bound.
You say you're satisfied but thoughts of fear await,
And when you think of death, you ask "What is my fate?"
Oh real and perfect strength is always found with Him,
No worries about tomorrow, His light is never dim.
Just when I think it's over, He always shows His face,
Giving me another day, filled with love and tender grace.
Now you think of all your friends, family members too,
And wonder how you can tell them, what Christ has done for you.
Just stop and count your blessings, name them one by one,
It surely will amaze them, what God has daily done.
Now strength, it is not purchased or requires a certain class,
Just simply come to Jesus, which is all the Savior asks.
Oh real and perfect strength, is always found with Him,
No worries about tomorrow, His light is never dim.
Just when I think it's over, He always shows His face-
Giving me another day, filled with love and tender grace.

"Starting a Family"

Written by R. Darryl Allgood

As a child, he seeks to remember, all the things he wished he had,
He cannot recall a home, to me that seems so sad.
He seeks to feel a history, a longing to be a part,
A union that is tied together, it is the longing within his heart.
Many years have passed him by now; he has grown into a man.
He wants to start a family, but does not how to begin.
The fear of all his childhood, the dark and dreary days,
It is almost like a ship at night, lingering in empty bays.
Just then, at the spur of a moment, a beam of light comes forth,
To direct the ship ashore, just turn and go due north.
This man has now a family, one he truly can adore,
He found the right foundation; it is God, the real and solid core.

"SUFFICIENT GRACE"

Written by R. Darryl Allgood

Elijah in the Bible was a man of great strength,
Everywhere he did travel, he spoke with great length.
He always pointing upward, lifting up God's dear name,
Jesus is the Savior; the reliever of your pain.
Great deeds and wondrous actions, works and miracles too,
All because of God's grace, a life was made anew.
Sufficient grace each morning, sufficient grace each night,
Everywhere that you travel, we are always in His sight.
Never a darkened moment, we are left along the side,
Sufficient grace each moment, sufficient grace abides.
Now David was a small one, not that big if you recall,
He faced the huge Goliath, and the giant took the fall.
So when you feel bewildered, walked and spat upon,
Just be another David; just trust the Holy one.
He holds the every star, the moon, the sun and space,
The wonder of it all, His unchanging Sufficient Grace.
Sufficient grace each morning, sufficient grace each night,
Everywhere that you travel, we are always in His sight.
Never a darkened moment, we are left along the side,
Sufficient grace each moment, sufficient grace abides.

"It Only Takes a Moment"

Written by R. Darryl Allgood

When it seems that you have traveled your last weary mile,
Your body is oh so tired and you want to rest awhile.
You glance for just one look to see if you are alone,
Then dial on heavens phone, you no longer want to roam.
You quickly get an answer; the voice is loud and clear,
There is no way question; you lose all sense of fear.
You can hear the angels singing, a peace of love divine,
The bells are loudly ringing the perfect timely chime.
He speaks with love so tender; a voice of care so true,
It has to me my father, he said "Child is that you?"
You finally dialed that number; you no longer want to wait,
You took the right road now, you see the golden gates.
It only takes a moment to make a phone call home,
It only takes a moment, are you tired of being alone?
He's always glad to hear, to talk or just be there,
It only takes a moment, your burden He wants to bear.
Don't ever be alarmed, frightened or just dismayed,
It only takes a moment; he turns your night to day.

"THE MAN WE CALL DAD"

Written by R. Darryl Allgood

I look at my life and all that I have learned,
There is no doubt; it was what he had yearned.
The adding, subtracting, and all that relate,
Keeping in mind, there was no debate.
He tells of the times when life was so hard,
He served in the War, our country he did guard.
Home he did come, as a soldier and proud,
He fought for his country, as he spoke to the crowd.
Now forming and shaping was part of his life,
He was gifted and blessed as a finely tuned knife.
His hands so skilled, talented, and free,
Like the sails on a ship that is guided by the breeze.
His ability was unique, if already you do find,
He was the only one, God's amazing to design.
God's purpose, God's plan as only He knows,
To transform his talents and a family bestow.
Now the boys and the girls for his life did await,
To be fashioned and molded, like a huge wedding cake.
All detailed, precise, as one does with the brass,
He guided his family as the teacher in class.
Now my mind is so vivid, detailed, and clear,
For the one that we speak, to my heart is so dear.
He has flourished and prospered in the life he has known,
For his children and family, he truly has grown.
No greater a man, as I stand here so glad,
As the one I do speak, the Man We Call Dad

"THE ANSWER IS ON ITS WAY"

Written by R. Darryl Allgood

As a child goes to his parent and seeks a small request,
He is sure he knows the answer; he has given his very best.
They pause for just a moment, a pause before reply,
The child is somewhat nervous, afraid of their deny.
His dad looks through his glasses, smiles and says ok,
The child is so excited; the answer came today.
The answer is on its way, God promised he would supply,
The answer is on its way, it comes from up on high.
So do not hang your head, just lift your load and pray,
For God is on the throne, the answer is on its way.
Have you ever prayed a prayer, just waiting for God to answer?
It seemed so long a night, but you knew He was the master?
Did you pour your spirit out, with every ounce of strength?
Was it in the darkest night, no matter what the length?
Just follow God's direction; just follow the one divine,
He hears your every prayer; He said your prayers are mine.
The answer is on its way, God promised he would supply,
The answer is on its way, it comes from up on high.
So don't be tired and anxious, just lift your load and pray,
Just shout with great excitement, the answer could come today.

"GOD'S BEAUTY"

Written by R. Darryl Allgood

The Lilly of the valley, the bright and morning star
He is the great creator; though I am near or oh so far.
The mountains and the sunset, the colors of the skies;
When you think that no one loves you and you question "Oh Lord why?"
Just take one glimpse of Calvary, the cross it will reveal;
There is no one, no other; His love is oh so real.
He's the rose of every morning, the star of every night;
The highest of every mountain and the brightest of every light.
Much deeper than any sea, far greater than any space;
God's beauty is far above any problem we ever face.
God's plan we often ponder and do not comprehend;
We go through many problems; our hearts He always mends.
We pray and search the scriptures; we look to Him for strength;
Our path has now been cleared, all done without a blink.
So when you feel no beauty, no care, no love or call;
Just look at all He's made; God's beauty is all in all.

"TAKE ONE STEP"

Written by R. Darryl Allgood

The grandest old story of years gone by;
Still holds to that power from up on the high.
Lives changed, made whole and turned all around;
He takes a broken home and sends them heaven bound.
It only takes His love; so real and undefiled;
Regardless of the mess; no matter how wild.
Take one step towards the cross of Calvary;
He'll do all the rest, it's called the victory.
Take one step toward the Savior today;
You will never regret, He never turns away;
God's power stands tall, above all the rest;
Just take one step and He will clean up your mess.
Yes, one, only one, yes a very little step;
As you travel in this world and you see all that's tossed.
Don't let Satan rob you, for they too, are the lost;
Not knowing their heavy burdens or all that they bear;
Their tears that are shed, nor the heartache that they wear.
Remember that day, when you too, first heard?
Your life was all broken, your spirit was stirred.
You took a step towards Jesus, you followed the path He lead;
Your life He has now has altered; All simply for being fed.
You grip that seat beside you; you run and hide your face;
But the Spirit is still knocking, simply because of wondrous grace.
So now let me remind you of a lost and dying place;
His arms are now wide open; no matter what your race.

"HIS TOUCH"

Written by R. Darryl Allgood

A Man was on his journey to place he'd never been;
He'd heard it's one of gladness, for you see, there is no sin.
This man had never spoken, not even "how are you?"
People would ignore him; they knew not what to do.
He spent his life for others; always giving himself;
He never asked one thing; always knew how others felt.
Always real quiet, never speaking you could say;
He finally met the master; oh what a wondrous day.
It only took His touch to make a blind man see;
It only took His touch; to save a soul like me.
Though sails are oh so torn and the skies are oh so dark;
His touch is the one—that mends your broken heart.
So release from that seat; your hands to now so clutch;
You will never, no never regret; being touched by His touch.
Now this man has grown old and many he has led;
To that cross on the hill where they put down their beds.
Now crippled and aged in the body below;
Not able to speak but humble I know.
Once able to stand with courage and strength
A witness for God he surly was meek.
As he stepped into Heaven, he had so very much;
When asked what the secret, it was His very touch.

"OUR PAIN"

Written by R. Darryl Allgood

When your body is weak and feeble, it gives pain that feels so bad,
When your life seems all forgotten, you cannot think happy, only sad.
When life's train comes rushing by you as it hurries upon its way,
It carries a load of purpose, just what I cannot say.
Be thankful as we travel, upon our weary road,
For soon, we will be standing at the place we will unload.
As we look beyond our life, at the river we all must cross,
Be thankful for the narrow path, for God we never lost.
So as you sit and ponder, you weigh your body's pain,
It really does not matter; Eternal life will be our gain.

ESSENTIAL AND HELPFUL TOOLS:

This section is designed to give you direction on how to study the Word of God with essential tools to help you to understand God's Word. Be careful to select books that are doctrinally sound so that you aren't steered in the wrong direction.

❖ *A Good Bible* that is the closest to the original manuscripts. There are so many versions that claim to be the best so seek out wisdom and direction from your pastor, youth leader or your Sunday school teacher. Don't be too quick to buy one without knowing what it is you are getting.

❖ A Bible Dictionary is one that will give you the definition of words that can seem hard to understand or define.

❖ A *Concordance* is included in many Bibles, but not in all of them. It is a book that list alphabetically the words used in the Bible with all the scripture references where they can be found. This is a very good Bible study tool.

❖ *A Bible Atlas* is a very good tool to have when you are reading or studying a certain geographical area in the Bible. It will visually help you see where they are talking about.

❖ *Commentaries* are very good to have and I thrive on them. I have my favorites and the ones I would recommend but seek advice from your pastor, youth leader or Sunday school teacher.

CPSIA information can be obtained at www.ICGtesting.com
Printed in the USA
LVOW130137100712

289388LV00002BA/1/P

9 781449 756062